COMING BACK FROM COVID

The Definitive Guide for Small Business Owners
to Rapidly Recovery From the Coronavirus

Evian Gutman

This book is dedicated to healthcare workers the world over. Your unrelenting commitment to patient care helped us get through the pandemic—even when coming at great personal sacrifice.

Thank you.

Contents

Preface

When the Coronavirus virus first reared its ugly head towards the end of 2019, it was initially contemplated with an abstract fascination as a phenomenon taking grip in lands far away.

In our thinking at the time, we remembered that we'd experienced all this before… *SARS* in 2002. *Swine Flu* in 2009. *Ebola* in 2014.

Except, we hadn't.

With its calamitous speed of infectious spread coupled with its high mortality rate; COVID-19 wreaked havoc across the globe—impacting every facet of life as we knew it and leaving none unaffected.

Health implications were naturally priority number one—taking care of yourself, your loved ones and society at large was the first order of affairs. With so many unknowns, and no vaccine at hand, uncertainty in how best to respond took afoot.

As if out of a textbook, the world looked as though it was going through the seven stages of grief: *shock, denial, anger, bargaining, depression, testing;* and then finally, *acceptance.*

But what had we come to accept?

We accepted that *societal norms* were no longer what they once were: maintaining a 'social distance' of six feet between yourself and others was now the new normal.

We accepted that *consumer expectations* were shaped by forces greater than simple market demand: no longer could you just go to the supermarket and expect to find toilet paper on the shelves.

We accepted that *civil liberties* were not absolute: being 'locked down' in your home and forbidden from leaving might be a justifiable trade-off for the public good of 'flattening the curve'.

We accepted that *working arrangements* were largely a legacy of convention: working from home and teleconferencing technologies could prove equally effective in fulfilling many day-to-day tasks.

And importantly, we accepted the *fragility of the assumptions* upon which many small businesses were built: the flaws in assuming that prior circumstances were reliable indicators of future prosperity.

Small businesses started to quickly feel the pinch. Money flowed out faster than it flowed in. Operations slowed down as demand evaporated, and funds to pay salaries dried up at similar speeds. Customers disappeared, and those that remained had less money to spend. COVID regulations were introduced that literally separated businesses from their customers.

Many good businesses that had weathered prior storms suddenly found themselves in the eye of a tornado with no escape plan in sight. Even as restrictions lightened, scar tissue from these impacts added salt to the wound.

COVID upended entire economies, industries, supply chains, consumer behaviors and finances in ways that prevented a return to 'business-as-usual' and life as it was once known. Pressures on small business owners became heavy and immense.

Working within this reality, it's tempting to put one's hands up in the air and simply throw in the towel. After all, most of these impacts are a consequence of externalities that were outside your control—not a function of your business' potential or stewardship.

However, do not discount the control you *still* maintain for running a high-performing and profitable business. As Winston Churchill famously said...

Never let a good crisis go to waste.

The coronavirus is a crisis you did not invite. It resulted in consequences you do not want. It threw into question many past recipes for success.

Yet the silver lining is that this crisis represents an opportunity to step-up your game. It represents a chance to address all the imperfections in your business that you've continually avoided up till now. *Now* is the time to revisit old assumptions and see if there's a better way of doing things. This unique moment represents an excuse to consider previously non-existent opportunities that align with new operating realities.

Many things are outside your control, but many things still remain *within your control* too...

Outside Your Control...	Within Your Control...
Financial Stress	Cash Flow Management
Social Lockdowns	New Distribution Channels
Weak economy	Developing New Markets
Industry Downturns	Product Innovation
Laws and Regulations	Access to Assistance Measures
Reduced Consumer Demand	Repeat Customer Business
Supply Chain Disruptions	Process Improvements
Less Access to Capital	Sales Force Effectiveness
Salary Constraints	Employee Incentives
Economy Recovery Timelines	Business Planning

Now is the time to recalibrate focus from *crisis management* to *business re-building*.

The business owners most likely to succeed will be those that are looking towards the horizon and preparing for this voyage.

Whilst COVID-19 was the crisis that nobody asked for, it stands to become the trigger for your future growth, profitability and prosperity.

For *adversity* is simply *opportunity*, in disguise.

How to Use This Book

Embarking on your post-COVID recovery is a daunting task.

The last time you had this many challenges hovering above your head may have been when you first started your business.

The *bad news* is, there's a lot to get right. The *good news* is, there's a lot to get right!

This book is your starting point for that journey. It contains a collection of high-impact, immediately-actionable strategies, tips and techniques for recovering your business from the impacts of COVID.

The book is broken down into six chapters:

Marketing and Sales   Product   Growth   Operations   Team   Accounting and Finance

Each chapter contains five initiatives, and each initiative is broken down further into ten practical tips for bringing each to life.

All businesses differ in a multitude of ways. Different *businesses* of different *sizes* exist in different *places* and at different *stages* of their organizational maturity. Inevitably, some tips will be more pertinent for your business than others.

The goal in using this book is to build yourself a recovery roadmap via a broad range of business initiatives. Each of these will require a dose of individual color and context to bring them to life, that reflect *your* unique operating realities.

Keep a notepad alongside you as you read through the book. Jot down ideas that come to you as you flick through the chapters, and bounce your ideas off others within your team too.

And when you feel overwhelmed by just how much there is to get right, remind yourself once again, of just how much there is, to get right!

Marketing and Sales

Understand Your New Customers With Buyer Personas

Target Customers With Inbound Marketing Tactics

Expedite Results With Pay Per Click Advertising

Reacquaint Yourself With Your Sales Pipeline

Develop Repeatable Results With Sales Playbooks

Understand Your New Customers With Buyer Personas

Sales represent the engine of your business, and the ability to make sales hinges on the value you provide to your customers. But who is your *customer*? And what do we actually mean by *value*?

Firstly, there is no generic 'customer'.

There is *Bob*—the dentist, with three kids, a mortgage, who enjoys sailing on weekends. There is *Lucy*—the grandmother, who depends on her pension and likes Italian food. And there is *Arthur*—the student, who lives at home with his parents and is saving his money to buy a popular video game.

Each of these customers have distinct backgrounds, personalities and interests. The combination of these defining attributes shape how effectively a given marketing message will resonate with them and when their personal buying drivers get activated.

Thinking about a generic customer for your marketing and sales efforts through a one-size-fits-all prism runs the risk of diluting these nuances that can be the difference between customers buying or not.

Now more than ever, traditional assumptions you might have held about your customer may be obsolete. Following COVID, there are new realities that everyone must contend with. These apply *especially* to your customers.

Your customers may carry new pain points that need to be addressed. They may possess new value drivers that need to be considered. They may act according to new behaviors and preferences that need to be recognized.

Building a richer understanding of your customers is the logical starting point for navigating through these challenging times.

Doing so is best achieved by creating *buyer personas*. These are fictitious avatars of your target customers that help you conceptualize them as real human beings with individualized needs and wants.

Buyer personas flip your modus operandi...

FROM	**TO**
Working backwards to retrofit your business' offering onto customer needs	Thinking forwards about your customer's needs to develop aligned offerings

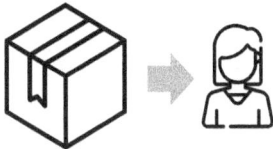

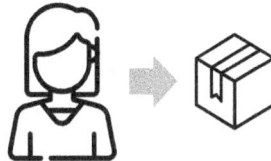

Buyer personas help you to better understand your customers—their pain points, wants and needs. They enable you to make better business decisions that cascade through all functions of your business.

Name: Jane Doe	**Occupation:** Physiotherapist
Age: 35	**Family:** Married, one child
Location: Miami, U.S.	**Languages:** English, Spanish

BIO

Jane runs a small physiotherapy clinic close to her home. She employs two part-time staff. She recently had a child and finds being a new parent that has returned to work challenging. Jane especially misses socializing with friends. She lives an active lifestyle, but finding time for personal exercise is difficult. She relies on social media to stay connected with friends and family.

GOALS

- Live active, social and healthy lifestyle
- Purchase a home close to the beach
- Lots of travel in near future

FRUSTRATIONS

- Work-life balance
- Challenges of healthy eating
- Personal finance challenges

PERSONALITY

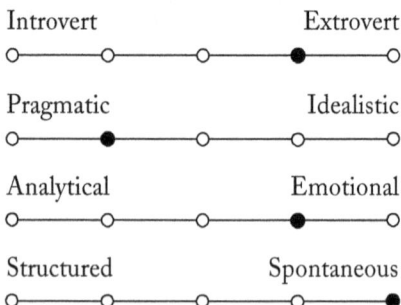

Introvert — Extrovert

Pragmatic — Idealistic

Analytical — Emotional

Structured — Spontaneous

LIKES

Brands

Platforms

Interests

So, how do you build buyer personas to better understand new and existing customers—who may have changed recently as a result of COVID?

Understand the Attributes You're Looking to Capture

Your goal in developing buyer personas is to build a composite 360° snapshot of your target customers. These illustrative avatars should feel as 'real' as possible: what do they look like? Where do they shop? What are their hopes and aspirations?

Remember... a lot of these things may be different now post-COVID, to what they previously once were. Use your personas to illuminate key *demographic*, *psychographic* and *behavioral* attributes, such as:

- Beliefs
- Background
- Consumer preferences
- Frustrations
- Goals

- Hobbies
- Interests
- Personality
- Predispositions
- Work ethic

Build Multiple Personas for Different Customer Profiles

It is unlikely you have only *one* type of buyer, so it makes sense to segment your customers into different customer profiles. Without going overboard, each persona should be markedly different, to capture unique attributes that indicate their personal buying drivers...

Bob the *Dentist*   Lucy the *Grandmother*   Arthur the *Student*

If buyer personas are to maintain relevance and utility, limit development to the smallest number of personas that still capture the diversity of your different customer profiles.

Conduct Customer Interviews

If you're looking to develop buyer personas that mirror your real-life customers, then the easiest way of going about achieving that goal is to *actually* speak with your real-life customers.

Request the opportunity to interview individuals that you believe represent your quintessential target customers. In the absence of face-to-face customer interviews, consider gathering information via online surveys or questionnaires.

Involve Your Team

After the *customer* themselves, there are few who understand the customer better than your team members. Across almost all business functions, team members deal with customers one way or another—some with high frequency and multiple touchpoints.

Make sure to involve key team members that are able to provide insight on the customer—especially those within the *marketing*, *sales* and *product* functions.

Undertake Independent Research

Supplement your customer interviews and team discussions with independent research too. Understand macro changes resulting from COVID that might be unearthed with fresh research and inquiry. This involves some good old-fashioned market research, like...

- Examining market reports
- Reading consumer review sites
- Analyzing your web analytics data

Aggregate Your Research and Interviews

Once you've collected these inputs, you'll be sitting on a ton of customer insights. That information needs to be consolidated and categorized into a meaningful structure to make it as easy as possible to build your personas. Group and summarize information into relevant categories, to make it simple and easy to transfer insights directly into respective personas:

Build a Solid Template

There are many ways to skin a cat and there's no 'right way' to build a buyer persona template. So long as you're guided by the overarching goal of gaining a snapshot that's representative of your real-life target customers, then the template attributes you decide to include should simply be those deemed necessary for achieving that objective.

Your persona templates should illuminate insights that help paint an illustrative picture of your target customer. They should empower you to feel capable of explaining the customer to someone as if they were a *real person* you knew in *real life*. Having a solid template will prove useful as you build multiple personas for use in making marketing and sales decisions that reflect your different customer profiles.

Humanize the Abstract

Endeavour to include humanizing elements into your template. This helps translate your 'abstract' research into a lifelike avatar. Conceptualizing your customers with these humanized attributes will prove handy when it comes time to using your personas for making real-world marketing and sales decisions.

Inevitably, your personas will not represent *every* customer that's relevant to your business—there will be natural variance from customer-to-customer. However, working with personas that feel like real human beings will make the decisions you make more authentic and reliable.

Be Specific

Be as specific as possible when building your personas. For example, if Jane wants to *live a healthy lifestyle*, then her challenge isn't just "healthy eating"—it's "finding balance between being a working mom, eating nutritious food and socializing with friends". Ensure that your personas get to the crux of who the target customer is actually all about.

Embed into Your Business

Once developed, your personas should be socialized amongst the entire team to be embedded across all business functions. They should serve as the North Star for every business decision that involves your customers, especially for sales and marketing.

Now more than ever, having a crystal-clear understanding of the customer is critical to all that you do.

Target Customers With Inbound Marketing Tactics

In the past, marketing messages were delivered top-down to the public. Large sums of money were spent purchasing mass media placements, and success was contingent on hoping that the right person happened to come across your advertisement at the exact time it was put out on display.

This 'spray-and-pray' approach was expensive, impersonal and largely ineffective.

With the dawn of digital and mobile technologies, a new type of marketing has emerged. *Inbound marketing* flips this approach on its head by having *customers* come to the business, rather than the *business* going at the customer.

It does this by scattering relevant content that potential customers are looking for, in all of the places they're looking to find it. Customers then interact with this content, which serves as a trigger for further engagement, and often culminates in a purchase.

'Push' Interruption Marketing
(the *old* way)

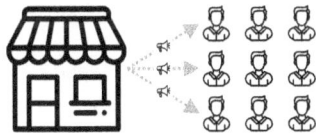

'Pull' Inbound Marketing
(the *new* way)

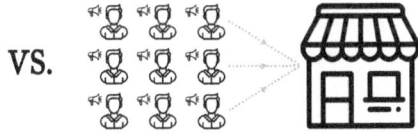

VS.

In short, inbound marketing tries to deliver the *right* content, to the *right* person, at the *right* time. When these stars align, marketing goals are frequently realized.

When times are tough, *marketing* often falls in the cross-hairs of cost-cutting measures, as businesses fight an existential battle. They adopt a 'survival mode' mentality, and anything that does not result in creating immediate sales opportunities tends to face the chopping board first.

In our post-COVID reality, shrewd businesses are not looking to *eliminate* their marketing budgets—these businesses appreciate marketing's importance as a critical revenue driver. Instead, they focus on ways they're able to extract maximum value from the marketing dollars they *do* decide to spend.

Even if budgets need to be cut back, these businesses still look for opportunities to *do more with less*. This becomes possible with a considered *inbound marketing* strategy.

Why is inbound marketing effective, and what can it help you to achieve?

- Better quality leads
- Builds your brand
- Cost controllable
- Creates long-term relationships
- Enduring and cost-effective
- Establishes trust and credibility
- Fully measurable
- High return on investment
- Micro-targeting possibilities
- Satisfies customer expectations
- Saves you time
- Superior customer experience
- Timely and personalized
- Viral, sharable and scalable

If inbound marketing is the vehicle that takes you to your customers, then *content assets* are the gas that fuels the journey. Content assets are the marketing resources owned by your business that *help* individuals in ways that are aligned to your offering.

Content assets take many forms—they may be a blog post; they may be a video; they may be a case study. Basically, content assets are anything intended to attract a potential (or existing) customer to your business; to then demonstrate capability, establish relevance and build relationships. With enough content assets that span the different stages of a customer's buying cycle, you can create a lead-nurturing flow that supports them throughout every stage of their buying journey.

So, how do you go about targeting customers with an impactful inbound marketing strategy that's comprised of great lead nurturing content?

Identify Your Target Audiences With Buyer Personas

Before embarking on a journey to develop a suite of content assets, you first need to know *who* those resources are intended for. It's pointless investing in this process if the assets won't resonate with the recipient.

Working professionals have different wants and needs to *students* ...

Men and *women* often have different buying drivers and behaviors ...

And *millennials* use online platforms more frequently than *seniors*.

These differences matter. Use the *buyer personas* you previously developed to determine different customer profiles you plan to target.

23

Conduct a Content Audit

A *content audit* helps you determine the content assets you already have in your possession, and any gaps that need to be plugged. Different individuals will have different needs and requirements depending on the stage of the buying cycle they're currently at. Some content assets are better suited to specific stages of the customer buying cycle:

	Customer Goals	Relevant Content Assets
Awareness	*Education* • Understand problem • Undertake research • Identify options	Blog posts eBooks Industry reports Social media posts Whitepapers
Consideration	*Solutions* • Evaluate choices • Compare benefits • Envisage opportunities	Comparison tables Expert guides Podcasts Videos Webinars
Decision	*Selection* • Experience solutions • Consider advantages • Make purchase	Case studies Demos Free trials Reviews Testimonials

Your content audit should identify the various content assets you already possess within your business. This will enable you to line them up against the different buying cycle stages for each of your personas...

Persona	Content Assets for...		
	Awareness	Consideration	Decision

The purpose of these audits is to determine where you have gaps in your 'bank' of content assets, so that you are able to then plug them.

Identify Your 'Watering Holes'

Once you've determined your different buyer personas and conducted a content audit, you'll also want to identify the different 'watering holes' your personas congregate around.

Just like the hungry lion loiters by watering holes in wait for thirsty zebras to attack, so too should your content be pushed out to the places congregated most frequently by its intended recipients.

Your buyer persona research should help you identify all of the places you are likely to get found by a given persona.

In addition to the watering holes upon which your content is initially released, you should also think about supplementary channels it may be syndicated and re-purposed upon too. Aim to maximize your content's distribution reach as widely as possible.

 ## Determine Your Content Release Timelines

A good content strategy is not a moment-in-time event. It is planned and sustained activity that occurs in perpetuity. Part of developing your content strategy is deciding *when* you'll be releasing (and syndicating or re-purposing) your content into the public domain.

Will you be releasing content daily? Which assets will be released more frequently? Will some customers be targeted on a more persistent basis? These are just some of the questions you should ask yourself when determining your content release timelines. For example, you may release weekly blog posts, run monthly webinars, create quarterly industry reports and publish an annual whitepaper...

Weekly:

Monthly:

Quarterly:

Annually:

Map Out Your Consolidated Inbound Marketing Strategy

Your inbound marketing strategy combines all of the different elements you've just identified and determined:

Who		*What*		*Where*		*When*
	+		+		+	
Buyer Personas		Content Assets		Watering Holes		Content Release Timelines

Map out your inbound marketing strategy in a spreadsheet to give you a birds-eye-view of the entire plan...

DECEMBER

When	What	Where	Targeting
Tue 1st	Weekly blog post	🖥 Facebook Twitter	(persona)
Wed 2nd	Monthly Podcast	SoundCloud Facebook Twitter	(persona) (persona) (persona)
Thu 3rd	Social media posts	Facebook Twitter Instagram	(persona)
Fri 4th	Quarterly Industry Report	🖥 Twitter (icon)	(persona)
Mon 7th	Social media posts	Facebook Twitter Instagram	(persona)
Tue 8th	Weekly blog post	🖥 Facebook Twitter	(persona)
Wed 9th	Social media posts	Facebook Twitter Instagram	(persona)
Thu 10th	Social media posts	Facebook Twitter Instagram	(persona)
Fri 11th	White Paper #12	🖥 ✉ Twitter	(persona)
Mon 14th	Weekly blog post	🖥 Facebook Twitter	(persona)
Tue 15th	Monthly Email	✉	(persona) (persona) (persona)
Wed 16th	Social media posts	Facebook Twitter Instagram	(persona)
Thu 17th	Social media posts	Facebook Twitter Instagram	(persona)
Fri 18th	Monthly Webinar	🖥 ✉ Facebook	(persona)
Mon 21st	Weekly blog post	🖥 Facebook Twitter	(persona)
Tue 22nd	Social media posts	Facebook Twitter Instagram	(persona)
Wed 23rd	Social media posts	Facebook Twitter Instagram	(persona)
Thu 24th	Social media posts	Facebook Twitter Instagram	(persona)
Fri 25th	Christmas Email	✉	(persona) (persona) (persona)
Mon 28th	Weekly blog post	🖥 Facebook Twitter	(persona)
Tue 29th	Webinar Sign-Up Email	✉	(persona)
Wed 30th	Social media posts	Facebook Twitter Instagram	(persona)
Thu 31st	Social media posts	Facebook Twitter Instagram	(persona) (persona) (persona)

Develop Great Content

Now that you've determined *what* you need to deliver, to *whom*, *where* and *when*; you're able to 'work backward' and identify where you have gaps in your content assets that need to be plugged.

Always be mindful of who you're developing the content for and the purpose it is intended to fundamentally achieve—as discussed, different content will be relevant to different people at different times.

For each of your assets, the common goal is to progress a prospective customer down the sales funnel. If raising *awareness*, the goal should be advancement to *consideration*. If being *considered*, the goal should be progression towards making a *decision*. And if making a *decision*, the goal should be a *sale* with your business...

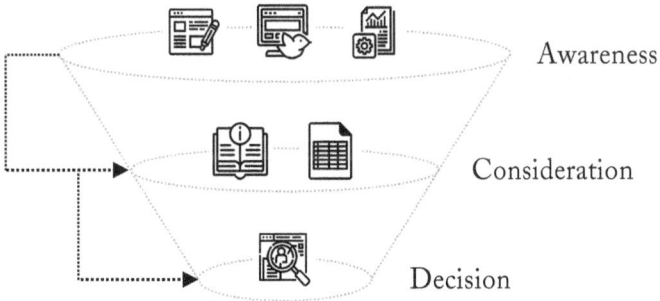

Awareness

Consideration

Decision

Back Your Content Up With Strong Call-To-Actions

Since the ultimate goal is a customer purchase, every asset of your inbound marketing strategy should be working towards that objective. Doing so requires progressing the customer through a series of pre-purchase stages with the support of relevant content at each and every one of those stages.

All assets therefore need a strong *call-to-action*. These are the explicit activities you want the individual to take as a matter of 'next steps'…

>> *Learn more with our webinar series*

>> *Still have questions? Call us for answers!*

>> *Try out our great products for yourself*

>> *Click here to see our solutions in action*

>> *Read what our customers have to say*

Deliver (and Syndicate) Your Content

Your investment in this process amounts to nothing if you drop the ball on execution. It is imperative that you remain disciplined in adhering to your mapped-out inbound marketing strategy. Ensure that you get your quality content into the hands of those that will appreciate and benefit from it.

In addition to releasing your content across its principally-intended channel, there may be opportunities to syndicate it amongst complimentary marketing channels too. This can be done at the same time it's initially released, or at any time in the future.

For example, to maximize exposure and derive optimal benefit, you may tweet to share a link back to a blog post you've just written for your website.

Repurpose Your Content

Since you've gone to the effort of developing great content, it would be a pity for those assets not to be utilized to their full potential.

A blog post on your website will be great for those that get to read it, but what about customers that 'loiter' around other 'watering holes' instead? Different customers prefer digesting content via different means.

In addition to publishing and syndicating your content, consider ways that you're able to re-purpose the same content into a new standalone asset. Examples include...

Converting a ...		Into a...
Blog Post	➡	Webinar
Industry Report	➡	Video
Whitepaper	➡	Infographic

During these post-COVID times, customers will be looking for help from multiple places. Ensure that you diffuse your presence as broadly as possible.

Nurture Your Leads

If we accept that the purpose of inbound marketing is to continuously provide relevant content that perpetually warms up an individual until a time that they're ready to buy, then it's important to adopt the mindset that inbound marketing is *not* just a moment-in-time exercise.

The goal of inbound marketing is to continually build upon your relationships with different individuals, and provide them with the particular assistance they desire at relevant times.

With lead nurturing, instead of going for a '*hard* sales close', you stand by the customer's side at every stage of their buyer's journey; and provide whatever support, information or assistance they require at any opportunity to do so.

By demonstrating *relevance, credibility* and *authority*, you'll become the natural choice when it does come time to pulling the pin and making a purchase. With the right lead nurturing strategy, you help the customer get to that point of purchase sooner.

A critical success factor is staying front-of-mind with potential customers. Not only will you be providing the 'education' piece, but you hope to provide the vital 'solution' piece too—the underlying reason you've gone to these efforts in the first place.

Maximize the number of customer 'touch-points' you're able to. Examples include...

- Automating emails
- Having an active presence on social media
- Scheduling follow-up courtesy calls

Marketing automation platforms, email marketing services, Customer Relationship Management (CRM) systems and social media management systems will all be incredibly useful in managing these processes. They perform most of the heavy lifting, automate many of the repetitive processes, and save you and your team a lot of time.

Expedite Results With Pay Per Click Advertising

COVID placed significant financial strain on businesses. It created dents in revenue projections, curtailed access to customers and opportunities for making sales.

There's no shortage of marketing tactics you're able to deploy when trying to connect with your customers. Why then, focus on Pay Per Click advertising?

Because Pay Per Click advertising is a 'shortcut' to results.

Pay Per Click internet advertising (often going by the names *Search Engine Marketing, Google Ads,* or *PPC* for short)—as the name suggests—works by displaying an online advertisement that charges you every time somebody clicks on it. These ads are displayed in the results of search engines or as banner advertisements on third party sites, that take individuals to your website when they click on your ads.

Unlike many other marketing tactics, the results are *immediate,* which is why it is so appropriate for plugging the holes left by COVID in your business *today.*

You may be asking, if it's so effective at achieving immediate results, why bother then with other marketing tactics at all—why not simply dedicate *all* marketing budget exclusively to Pay Per Click? The answer is that there's a trade-off between the *immediacy* and *permanence* of results.

Someone searching for "discount running shoes" on Google represents a potential customer with high purchase intent. It is no accident that they've typed *that* very search query at *that* very time into a search engine.

Show them an advertisement for discount running shoes in six months, and it will almost certainly be of far less relevance. PPC advertising therefore has a rapidly-depleting return on investment as time goes on, in ways that other more 'enduring' marketing tactics (e.g. Search Engine Optimization) do not.

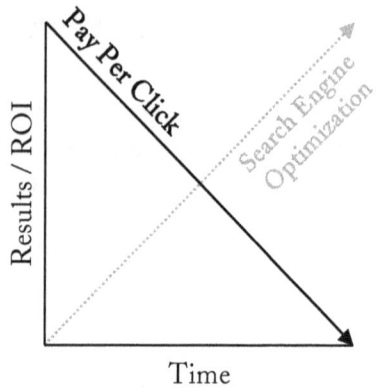

Why is Pay Per Click advertising especially relevant and useful in these post-COVID times?

☕ Quick and Simple
You're able to set up a PPC account and have your ads up and running in a matter of hours. Ads are then displayed instantaneously to customers.

🖥 Integral Component of the Buyer's Journey
70% of customers begin their buyer's journey with a web search. Without a prominent search engine presence, it's likely you'll get overlooked.

⏚ Qualified Leads
PPC allows you to identify high-level buyer intent and direct those individuals to your website to close the loop and make the sale.

⚲ Precise Targeting
You create your ad copy, decide who sees your ads, where and when ads get shown, and how much you're prepared to pay to have ads display.

Run Experiments and Track Results

All campaign results are trackable and reportable. Run tests and continually optimize to generate the highest converting traffic at the lowest possible cost.

Competitive Equalizer

Both the 'big boys' and 'little guys' are provided with the same opportunities to appear at the top of search results, making it a handy competitive leveller.

Cost Controllable

You decide how much to spend and on which campaigns. You only pay when somebody clicks, which makes it an efficient use of marketing budget.

So, how do you go about expediting results with Pay Per Click advertising?

Find the Right Keywords

Your keywords are the bridge between a customer's search query and your ad being displayed. Better keywords will improve your ad's relevance, increase its impressions and maximize conversion rates.

Start by brainstorming a list of keywords that you believe match *what you sell* with *what your customers are looking for.* You're able to get recommendations from tools like Google's Keyword Planner as well as other tools that help you look at your competitors' keywords too.

Have a good think about any post-COVID specific keywords that customers may be using. Include keywords that span the breadth of different keyword categories; like *branded keywords* (including your business' name), keywords that *indicate an intent to buy*, and *'long-tail' keywords* with longer—but more specific—search phrases...

> 🔍 discount running shoes

> 🔍 buy running shoes

> 🔍 running shoes

> 🔍 cheap running shoes

> 🔍 nike running shoes

> 🔍 ny shoe mall

> 🔍 where can i find cheap running shoes in ny

Make Use of 'Negative' Keywords

Negative keywords are keywords you specify that *prevent* your ad from being triggered for display when used in a search query. They matter because without negative keywords, your ads may display for unrelated or irrelevant search queries. These will dilute the effectiveness of your Pay Per Click campaigns and waste precious marketing dollars. For example...

If your restaurant sells *hamburgers*...

You'll want to get found for search queries like "hamburger restaurants"...

But not get found for search queries like "hamburger recipes"

Select the Optimal *Match Types*

The *match type* you select for your keywords will determine whether your ad gets triggered for display or not.

The default match type is *broad match,* and will trigger ads for searches that include the exact search query, misspellings, synonyms, related searches and other relevant variations.

Phrase match will trigger matches of the phrase with additional words before or after it too. For example, the search query "buy sneakers" would trigger an ad containing the keyword "sneakers".

Exact match will do exactly that—display your ad for the exact match of the search query (or close variations of that exact term with the same meaning).

Create Good Ad Copy

Having good ad copy is critical for effective Pay Per Click campaigns. Get this right and you'll flood your website with qualified potential customers. Get this wrong and you'll be pouring money down the drain.

Now's a great time to create ad copy that makes it explicit to customers that you appreciate their current post-COVID realities. A few things to keep in mind when creating ad copy...

- Highlight points of competitive differentiation
- Include a compelling call-to-action
- Make it personal by focusing on benefits
- Play to people's emotions
- Use relevant keywords throughout your ads

Develop Multiple Ads

When it comes to Pay Per Click, it's very much a case of trial and error—often the things you expect to work best don't perform as well as you'd hoped, and things you didn't expect to perform so well may smash the ball out of the park.

It's important therefore that you have multiple ads on rotation. Since Pay Per Click provides you with detailed reports and analytics, you're able to instantaneously see which ads were most effective.

With brief experimentation, you'll quickly be able to identify your most effective ads, and double-down on the ad copy that achieves the greatest cut-through.

Select the Right Bid Strategy

Your *bid strategy* is the approach you take for achieving a particular Pay Per Click goal. Maybe you're trying to…

Build brand awareness by amplifying ad impression displays

Get more clicks

Maximize goal conversions (e.g. filling out a contact form)

Once you're clear on your goal, you're able to specify your bid strategy and allow the Pay Per Click platform to optimize on your behalf to help you achieve your particular objective.

Target Specific Demographics

One of the beauties of Pay Per Click advertising is the ability to zone-in on precisely who it is you want to target. Pay Per Click advertising platforms enable you to selectively display your ads for a specific subset of potential customers, defined by their…

Age   Gender

Household income   Parental status

Do any of these demographics possess new post-COVID needs amongst your target customers?

In addition to reaching your target customers, you're also able to develop bespoke copy for individual ads that can be more appealing to the specific demographics for whom the ad is displayed.

Use Geo-Targeting

For many small businesses, *their* customers are confined to a specific geographical location. This may be a suburb, city, state or country.

Pay Per Click advertising platforms allow you to specify the locations that users must be in to see your ads. You're able to be as specific as targeting an individual zip code, or as broad as selecting (or excluding) individual countries.

By using these geo-targeting features, you prevent precious advertising dollars from being wasted on delivering ads to individuals that were never going to become customers in the first place. And just like with targeting specific demographics, you're able to develop tailored ad copy that's intentionally written for customers in select locations.

Take Advantage of Device Targeting

Not too long ago, it would have been fair to say that most internet searches took place sitting down at a desk in front of a computer.

That is no longer the case. Mobile internet usage has resulted in a surge of internet searches taking place on-the-go. For small local businesses, having your ads displayed on people's mobile devices can make a world of difference to the results you see from Pay Per Click.

Now that lockdowns are over, make sure that your ads take advantage of device targeting for *desktop, mobile* and *tablets* to get found by the right customers in the right contexts at all the right times.

Use Call Campaigns to Encourage Immediate Contact

Why send someone to your website if all they really want to do is simply speak to you on the phone straight away?

Eliminate making potential customers jump through this extra hoop by creating call campaigns that encourage them to call you directly from your ad on the search engine results page...

They show only on mobile devices and can be set to display exclusively during the times that your business is open and able to take calls.

Reacquaint Yourself With Your Sales Pipeline

Your sales pipeline is a snapshot of all of the opportunities that could result in a sale in the near future. It breaks these opportunities down into relevant stages that indicate timelines till close and the likelihood of the sale happening...

Opportunity	Entered	Stage	Size	Probability	Weighted Size
1st Quarter					
Company A	JAN	Presentation Scheduled	$40,000	60%	$24,000
Company B	FEB	Qualified Opportunity	$50,000	40%	$20,000
Company C	MAR	Appointment Scheduled	$20,000	20%	$4,000
1st Quarter Totals:			$110,000	-	$48,000
2nd Quarter					
Company D	APR	Decision Maker Involved	$50,000	80%	$40,000
Company E	MAY	Presentation Scheduled	$20,000	60%	$12,000
Company F	JUN	Qualified Opportunity	$100,000	40%	$40,000
2nd Quarter Totals:			$170,000	-	$92,000

Prior to COVID, the predictability of sales and their timelines were better known. Unfortunately now, there are fewer certainties, and assumptions are less reliable.

Your sales pipeline is useful for distinguishing different sales opportunities. Some will be *large* and some will be *small*. Some will be *won* and some will be *lost*. Some will have *immediate* timelines and some will be *drawn-out*. In addition to appreciating the total potential 'size-of-the-prize', these distinctions enable you to prioritize your sales efforts around the biggest, most profitable and probable opportunities.

Having an accurate sales pipeline will assist with your post-COVID recovery by improving your...

- Cash flow management
- On-target performance
- Sales performance
- Sales processes
- Stagnating sales
- Time-to-close timelines

These all become important as you try to rebound from the impacts of COVID and put your business back onto a path of stability. Frequent review of an up-to-date pipeline will help you keep a finger on the pulse of your business, identify issues before they hit crisis-point and maximize the likelihood of success for both obvious and less obvious opportunities.

So, how do you go about building a solid sales pipeline framework?

Define Your Pipeline Stages

Defining stages for your sales pipeline lays the foundations for progressing opportunities towards a sale in a pragmatic and methodical way. It breaks down the complexity involved in big or drawn-out deals by providing a paint-by-numbers roadmap for getting from start to finish without losing focus of the goal.

Common deal stages for big opportunities typically include:

1. Appointment Scheduled
2. Qualified Opportunity
3. Presentation Scheduled
4. Decision Maker Involved
5. Contract Sent
6. Closed - Won
7. Closed – Lost

You may wish to add additional stages if this will help you better manage your own opportunity progressions.

However, it's important not to overcook your sales process by adding too many stages to your sales pipeline. You should include only the minimum number of stages required to capture the different progression points that convert a lead at the top of your sales funnel into a customer down at the bottom.

Prioritize Your Opportunities

Your sales pipeline should show you all the information you need to understand each of the opportunities within your business that are on-the-go. This includes how much you stand to make, the age and stage of the opportunity and the likelihood of closing the deal.

Armed with this knowledge, you're able to prioritize your opportunities and mobilize resources accordingly. For example, a high-value low-probability deal at the top of the funnel may be deemed less important than a low-value, high-probability deal at the bottom of the funnel.

Would you have come to a different conclusion prior to COVID? Maybe. However, your pipeline ensures it is now made purposefully, and grounded in facts.

Weed Out Opportunities Unlikely to Convert

Doing regular reviews of an accurate pipeline will thrust each opportunity under the microscope. In prioritizing these opportunities, you'll be forced to ask hard questions around the likelihood of each opportunity progressing further.

If an opportunity is unlikely to convert and is taking your time away from other opportunities with greater promise, then consider removing them from your pipeline or parking them for an appropriate time to be re-visited again in the future.

Update Your Pipeline Tracking Tools Frequently

Depending on your requirements, you may choose to track opportunities in something as basic as a spreadsheet, or as sophisticated as a CRM system.

Whatever tool you choose, make sure that it is updated *frequently*. The quality of your tracking tool's outputs will only be as good as the quality of their inputs. If those inputs are not accurate, reliable or current; then the decisions you make off the back of these tools' insights will be equally inaccurate, unreliable or stale.

In our post-COVID reality, you simply can't afford to be operating without accurate sales information.

Track Relevant Opportunity Information

It's critical that you keep excellent records for all live opportunities. It is inevitable that you won't remember every conversation you have or piece of intelligence you pick up along the way.

You therefore need a singular 'source of truth' that's known as the go-to destination for anything and everything to do with all live opportunities. This is best done with a CRM system, though as noted, can also be achieved with less sophisticated pipeline tracking tools, like spreadsheets too.

Track key opportunity intel you've picked up, next-step commitments and any additional information that helps you maintain sales momentum and healthy customer relationships.

You'll thank yourself later when attempting to progress the opportunity.

Build a Sales Dashboard

The principle benefit of re-acquainting yourself with your sales pipeline is to make better decisions. Ensure that your pipeline includes a sales dashboard that gives you a macro snapshot of all the opportunities on-the-go, insights on how to progress them and forecasts on the likelihood of success.

Sales Pipeline	Key Opportunities	Forecast by Month
Individual Pipelines	Quota Attainment	Opportunity Types

Your dashboard should be dynamic to ensure that it is always accurate and should include your core sales KPIs and metrics.

Automate Elements of Your Sales Processes

The principle goal of the sales pipeline is to progress opportunities forwards as quickly and efficiently as you're able to. With that being the case, look towards automating as many processes that work towards achieving this goal as you can.

A good starting point is using marketing automation tools that automatically send out templated emails to specific contacts upon triggering events, like a pipeline stage update in your CRM system.

In this way, you're able to deliver targeted messages to relevant contacts without you or the team needing to manually do much of the heavy-lifting yourself.

Run Regular Sales Pipeline Meetings

It's important to give your team regular updates on the status of the pipeline and the business' priorities in pursuing live opportunities. These meetings are an essential ingredient in creating a culture of collective ownership for the business' performance.

Only through running regular sales pipeline meetings is everyone able to get on the same page to make dynamic, business-wide decisions that impact the time, energy and resources needed to be invested in pursuing various opportunities.

Become Perpetually Fixated With Next Steps

The secret to sales pipeline progression is controlling the process. As long as you're in the driver's seat commanding next steps, there's reduced risk of opportunities collapsing or being lost.

Be crystal clear on any action items for yourself, your team, key contacts and decision-makers involved in opportunities. Be explicit around timelines and commitments. Follow-up everything *you're* able to take care of on your end as expeditiously as possible. Address outstanding undertakings that are impeding opportunity progression.

Whereas previously, you may have had the luxury of taking your time to expedite opportunities, post-COVID realities have injected new urgencies into many scenarios. The more ownership of next steps *you* take on board, the more control of the process you'll maintain.

Use as a Cash Flow Forecasting Tool

COVID created big strains on cash flow for businesses. Now more than ever, businesses need to be on top of where their next dollar is coming from, and when that's going to happen. An accurate sales pipeline increases the visibility and predictability of your cash flows.

Attach *probabilities* and *values* to different opportunities at different stages of your pipeline to help with your cash flow forecasting.

Opportunity Stage	Probability
🗓 Appointment Scheduled	20%
🗨 Qualified Opportunity	40%
🖼 Presentation Scheduled	60%
👥 Decision Maker Involved	80%
📝 Contract Sent	90%
🏆 Closed – Won	100%
🏛 Closed - Lost	0%

Develop Repeatable Results With Sales Playbooks

Across every business, there are often stand-out team members that outperform the rest of their team. These high-performers possess the right mindsets, exhibit noteworthy skills and achieve superior results. They are often the trailblazers for creating winning processes that you wish the rest of the team adhered to, to achieve similar outcomes.

Sales playbooks are an attempt to capture and bottle those sales best practices. They are intended to serve as a repository of information that enable your team to *sell more*, with *greater ease* and *increased frequency*.

Now more than ever, your business must focus on getting down to business and delivering results. Unlike better times, the room for error is lower, and everyone needs to perform at the peak of their game. You need an *entire team* of high-performers, and the easiest way of creating that is by replicating the proven methods of success.

What are some of the components that sit in a sales playbook?

Buyer personas	Product overviews
Call scripts	Proposal guidelines
Company overview	Questions to ask
CRM best practices	Resources
Examples	Sales processes
KPIs	Sample meeting agendas
Messaging	Template emails

Since your sales playbooks will become the definitive go-to reference for sales best practices within your business, you'll want to ensure you've got everything spot-on, and not set your team down a wrong path.

Here are some tips for developing your sales playbooks for repeatable results...

Involve the Whole Team

Your sales playbooks are a compilation of best practice. There are inevitably a select handful of your highest-performers that you'll want to bring into the fold when creating them. Chances are, these high-performers are scattered far and wide across your entire business. For this reason, make sure you involve as many team members as possible, with a specific focus on your *marketing*, *sales* and *product* teams.

Transfer Knowledge Out of the Heads of Individuals

In the absence of sales playbooks, it's *you* and your *team* that become the locus of best practice and the go-to destination for having sales-related questions answered. Whilst learning from others and team collaboration is by no means a bad thing; it isn't always practical, nor is it an efficient method of consolidating your business' know-how.

When your entire team have access to sales playbooks, you transfer this knowledge from the decentralized brains of individual team members into a singular arbiter of best practices that's available on-demand 24/7. With sales playbooks, there's no faffing around looking for sales aids that are known to exist (somewhere!?).

You'll also derive increased ROI from these aids; as more team members benefit, from more resources, more often. All of this amounts to increased productivity and more time for your team to focus on progressing opportunities.

Standardize Your Best Practices

Your high-performers serve as role models for the rest of your team. There's potential to elevate the results your business *could* achieve if everyone emulated the mindsets, behaviors and skills that they exhibit.

Your sales playbooks allow you to do just that. Through your playbooks, you're able to capture the secret sauce of their outperformance and standardize those best practices.

Your playbooks act as an all-encompassing reference, that minimize performance variance and allow others to replicate your high-performers' methods of success.

Right-Size Your Playbooks

Your business may sell different products to different customers in different ways. It may not be feasible to create a playbook that captures *everything* sales-related for the entire business in one single document.

In some instances, it may be more practical to create separate playbooks for specific purposes. For example, you could make a playbook for one of your product lines, a playbook for a specific product, and a playbook intended for use by select team members with specific role functions.

Think about the areas of your business most gravely impacted by COVID, and where it might make greatest sense to dedicate any playbook development focus.

Collate all of Your Existing Marketing and Sales Collateral

Your sales playbooks are supposed to represent the ultimate source of truth for everything that's sales-related. Over the years you and your team would no doubt have developed an array of sales aids and resources that are probably in use today.

Building sales playbooks is an opportunity to stocktake all of these resources and consolidate them under the umbrella of your playbooks. There may be elements of duplication and things flagged as in need of an update. This is by no means problematic—in addition to centralizing everything you have; you're also able to determine what's *good*, what's *irrelevant*, and what needs a *refresh*.

Map Your Sales Process to the Customer's Buying Cycle

In the excitement of documenting your sales process and capturing internal best practices, it's easy to forget what this is all ultimately about: winning more sales with customers. You therefore cannot build your playbooks without first considering the *customer's buying cycle*.

The customer's buying cycle explains...

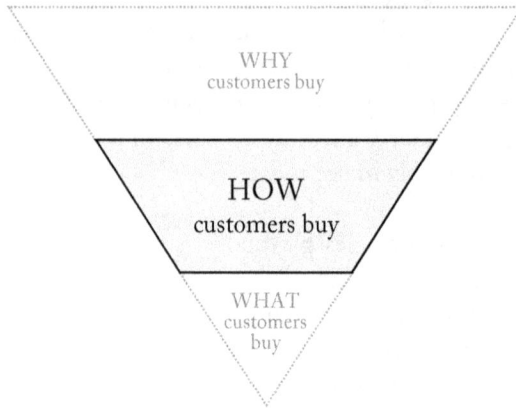

WHY
customers buy

HOW
customers buy

WHAT
customers
buy

COVID altered many things, including ways in which customers buy. It's critical you're familiar with changes to customer buying patterns.

To avoid building your playbooks in a vacuum, think about the different stages of the customer buying cycle from the perspective of the buyer personas you previously built. Consider the different stages a customer goes through before making a purchase, then map your sales process to each of those stages...

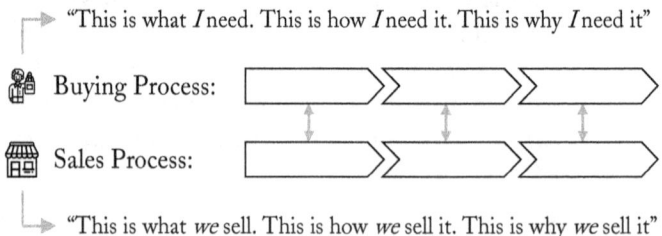

"This is what *I* need. This is how *I* need it. This is why *I* need it"

Buying Process:

Sales Process:

"This is what *we* sell. This is how *we* sell it. This is why *we* sell it"

Use for Onboarding

Think about what's involved in onboarding a new team member: you scour the business to piece together everything and anything that might prove relevant or handy in bringing the new hire up to speed on how to perform their role. This not only wastes a lot of time, but is an ineffective way of tapping the business's know-how.

Use this time right now to prepare the business for its return to hiring and onboarding in the future. Capture best practices, prepare your sales playbooks, and have your ducks lined up to make future onboarding processes as seamless and fruitful as possible.

Support With Training

Once you've developed your playbooks, it's important to remember that the job is not yet complete. You now possess the *map*, but it's time to go out looking for the *treasure*.

Utilizing the asset requires familiarizing the team with all the gold nuggets contained within its pages. Without the right communications, socialization and training to accompany the playbooks' launch; it's likely that their release will be a sizzle-then-fizzle event.

Capitalize on all the hard work that's gone into producing them. Transfer the knowledge that's contained within their pages back into the heads of the entire team.

Promote Adoption and Ease of Access

Beyond training, your sales playbooks are only as good as the extent that they're used. You play a pivotal role in promoting their adoption.

They need to become a living and breathing resource to the business, that's easily accessible at any point in time. The team should continually be pointed in their direction and reminded of the benefits they serve. Your playbooks need to be seen as a critical asset in your post-COVID recovery plan.

Take opportunities to reference your playbooks in different forums and meetings you're responsible for running. For example, playbooks could be referenced in a weekly sales meeting, where high-performers give an example of when the playbook was recently used, and the results that were achieved by doing so.

Update Periodically

As time goes on, things naturally evolve—be it your *industry, business* or *best practices.* For instance, the world we now live in is markedly different post-COVID than the world we lived in pre-COVID.

As the go-to reference for sales best practices, it's critical that your playbooks remain current and up-to-date. If team members start feeling like they are dated or irrelevant, they'll turn elsewhere to achieve everything that the playbook is supposed to help them to do. Those alternatives may not reflect vetted best practice and certainly won't be the most efficient way of acquiring the knowledge.

Schedule periodic reviews and updates of your playbooks. Ensure that the review and update process involves experienced and knowledgeable team members that are well-placed to validate currency, and provide additional updates if necessary.

Case Study: Marketing and Sales

Context

Judy runs a local travel agency.

When COVID hit; countries locked their borders, travel and hospitality ground to a halt, and about the only work left to be done was to cancel existing bookings. As a result, Judy had to furlough three-quarters of her team.

Recently however, the domestic travel industry has started to pick up once again, with customers looking to release their pent-up desires for some well-earned rest and relaxation.

Judy knows that the 'post-COVID' traveler is a different customer to before, but she is unsure of exactly how so.

Actions

Judy conducted customer interviews and spoke with her customer-facing team members to develop buyer personas that captured new psychographic attributes of her post-COVID target customers.

Her and her team developed great marketing content that promoted domestic travel. This was pumped out via blog posts and social media, after identifying these as being the most relevant channels to connect with the travel agency's target customers.

These marketing efforts were supported with Pay Per Click advertising on Google, which targeted families living within 50 miles of her business.

The business added a sales dashboard to their CRM to help track the progress of new enquiries. They also started sending automated marketing emails, based on a customer's stage in the sales cycle.

Judy notices that two-thirds of sales are coming from one-third of her team. She captures their 'secret sauce' in sales playbooks, that are then used for training the entire team now that staff have returned and been re-hired.

Results

Judy's travel agency develops a local reputation for being 'in-the-know' when it comes to travel destinations that have re-opened.

The business receives four times the enquiries from Google Ads than it previously did from ads placed in travel magazines.

Through tracking her sales pipeline, Judy is able to increase/decrease her monthly Pay Per Click budget to supplement the quieter months.

There is also an uptick and greater consistency in sales performance across the entire team.

Product

Optimize Your Product Mix

Maximize Profits With a Product Pricing Strategy

Re-Build Your Brand

Improve Your Offering With Better Customer Feedback

Cost-Effectively Differentiate Yourself on Quality

Optimize Your Product Mix

The unifying feature of all business types and sizes is the transactional exchange of their products for customers' money. Some businesses may only sell one thing. Other businesses may sell many.

Whilst it may intuitively seem that the more things you sell, the more opportunity exists to make more money, this isn't always the case...

← ↑ ↓ → In stretching yourself too *wide*, you may inadvertently dilute the quality of products you initially sold well. You also drain your finite production, marketing and sales resources away from your core product offerings. This may inadvertently result in customer dissatisfaction with products they formally once loved.

↓ → ↑ ← Conversely, focusing too *narrowly* may be prohibitive on realizing lucrative growth opportunities that line up nicely with your existing product offerings and capabilities. You may miss out on some simple—yet impactful—upsell or cross-sell opportunities. In so doing, you might fail to take advantage of profitable economies of scale.

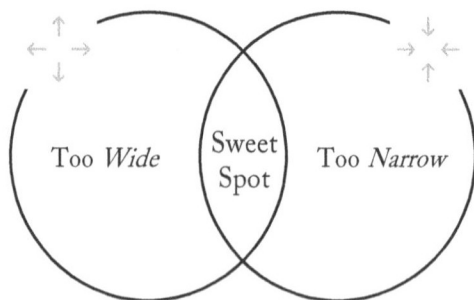

Too *Wide* | Sweet Spot | Too *Narrow*

COVID will have impacted many of the factors that influence finding your product mix *sweet spot.*

- Business strategy
- Competitive activity
- Consumer attitudes and behaviors
- Costs and quantities of production
- Finances and resourcing capacity
- Market demand
- Marketing capacity and capabilities
- Product profitability
- Regulatory environment
- State of the economy

Think about your current product mix as it exists today. Has it adapted in any way from pre-COVID to post-COVID times? What impacts, if any, has COVID had on the factors that influence your product mix sweet spot? What *new* factors need to be considered to account for changes resulting from COVID?

All these questions implore business owners to explore strategies for recalibrating their optimal product mix.

Before you do, it's important to understand a few key concepts and terms concerning the *product mix*:

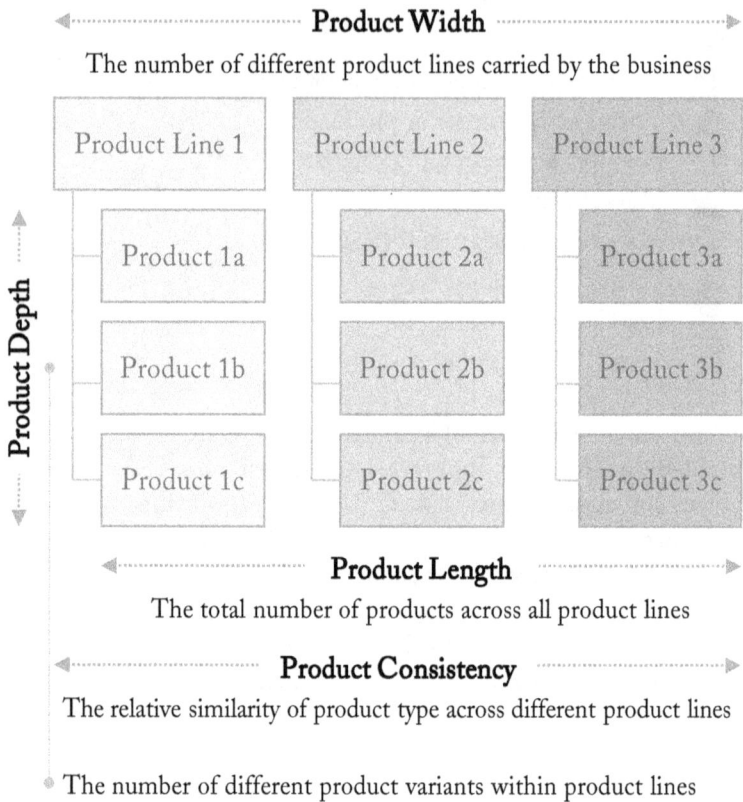

◄·· **Product Width** ································►

The number of different product lines carried by the business

Product Line 1	Product Line 2	Product Line 3
Product 1a	Product 2a	Product 3a
Product 1b	Product 2b	Product 3b
Product 1c	Product 2c	Product 3c

Product Depth (vertical axis label)

◄·· **Product Length** ·······························►

The total number of products across all product lines

◄··· **Product Consistency** ······················►

The relative similarity of product type across different product lines

• The number of different product variants within product lines

With these concepts in mind, let's explore some tactics at your disposal for optimizing your product mix...

Be Clear on Your Goals

Optimizing your product mix is difficult if you don't have a clear goal that you're trying to achieve. Align decisions that alter your product mix with considerations of your market objectives. Make sure to incorporate new market goals that were spawned by COVID.

For example, are you trying to win more customers? Are you trying to grow additional demand from an existing customer base?... Depending on your goal, there'll be different implications to decisions you make concerning your product mix strategy.

Review Your Existing Product Mix

Before making tweaks to your product mix, take a look at how it is currently composed today. For each of your products; understand historic sales volumes, costs of production and profitability. Make sure you understand the performance over time of these metrics, with a specific focus on comparing pre and post-COVID timeframes.

Armed with this knowledge, you'll be in an informed position to move forward and optimize your product mix.

Understand Your Production Costs

If you plan on modifying your product mix, you first need to have a good grasp on the implications—both good and bad—to your manufacturing and production costs of doing so.

For example, adding an entirely new product line may be outside your current financial means, but making a small variation to an existing product might be entirely possible.

There may also be significant cost savings to be won in scaling back your product mix—especially if production costs of certain lines are high but profitability remains low.

Consider Your Brand and Reputation

It's important to consider your brand and reputation when making adjustments to your product mix. You may be able to leverage your strong brand reputation for gaining market share with an expansion of your product mix.

However, be cautious against the consequences of spreading yourself too thin with too many products. This runs the risk of causing brand damage that is difficult to contain, and which may start to damage your otherwise good reputation.

Reconcile Short Term and Long Term Goals

Fight the temptation to implement knee-jerk alterations to your product mix in response to the COVID crisis.

There may be specific products previously perceived as pivotal to your business' future growth, but temporarily stunted by the impacts of COVID. Conversely, other products may have become your 'saving grace' throughout the crisis, even if they bear little weight on future growth objectives.

Make sure that you adopt a 'long-game' mentality when optimizing your product mix that balances your short-term realities with your long-term aspirations.

Expand or Contract Based on Balancing Considerations

There are multiple considerations that come into play when optimizing your product mix. Where you land will be a function of how these different factors intersect with one another. Ensure that any decisions to expand or contract your product mix considers...

Bandwidth and capacity	Brand reputation	General appetite

Market demand	Production costs	Resources and capabilities

Consider Natural Product Lifecycles

Making decisions that impact your product mix should not occur in a vacuum. In addition to the specific impacts of COVID, all products go through a natural lifecycle that should impact any decisions you make...

Introduction ➡ Growth ➡ Maturity ➡ Decline

Certain products within your mix might currently be in (or soon approaching) *maturity* and/or *decline*. If this is the case for your business, you need to ensure that *other* products in your product mix are able to compensate for resultant sales and/or profitability declines.

This may require elevating the prominence of certain products already within your mix, or adding new products entirely.

Scrutinize Margins in Addition to Sales Volumes

Different products have different levels of popularity. However, your best-sellers aren't always your highest-margin products. Choosing which products you wish to promote more heavily is a lever within your control.

You have the ability to ramp-up or ramp-down the extent to which you market select products. If COVID has reduced the volume of your sales, then it might be worth considering running marketing campaigns that shine a spotlight on products with better margins, until times improve.

Consider Implications to Messaging and Positioning

Expanding your product mix will have implications on the ways you market new products—it will rarely be a copy-and-paste job that simply replaces the words "Product A" with "Product B".

New products are likely to require bespoke product messaging and positioning that appeals to different customers than the product messaging and positioning used by your current product mix.

Regardless of what you decide to do, make sure that your product messaging resonates with customers living in a post-COVID world.

Productize Your Services

Not every business sells purely 'tangible' products. Even those that do may sell less-tangible service offerings in addition to their physical products too.

Maybe you've added a 'service' element to your products as a result of COVID and wish to maintain this as a permanent feature of your offering.

There's often substantial intrinsic value in many of these services that don't get monetized because of the challenges of communicating value for *services*, as distinct from products.

Productizing your services is one way of capturing this value to enable adding it to your product mix. It involves documenting the service, the time and resources that go into them, and the deliverables or outputs that materially benefit the customer.

When all of this is spelt out and itemized, intrinsic value is more easily and explicitly communicated.

Maximize Profits With a Product Pricing Strategy

The prices you set are not arbitrary. For many businesses, prices are simply determined using the 'cost-plus' model of adding a fixed margin on top of operating costs. But in addition to this simplistic approach, there are many other product pricing strategies you're able to deploy to maximize profits.

However, deploying the *right* pricing strategy involves walking a delicate tightrope... Price *too high* and you'll discourage potential customers from purchasing your products. Price *too low* and you'll miss out on untapped revenue opportunities. Adding a further layer of complexity, there are also branding considerations to consider around how you want customers to perceive your products too.

Striking the optimal balance requires having a solid familiarity of your...

Costs	+	Customers	+	Goals	+	Market	+	Products

In these difficult times, it may feel logical to plug revenue gaps by acquiring new customers. However before tasking yourself with this challenging job, first ask yourself whether you're able to extract any untapped value from your existing customers, which can typically be achieved at lesser cost and with great reward.

Extracting maximum customer value whilst keeping acquisition costs low is a function of how you *monetize* customers. And how you monetize customers is a function of your *pricing strategy*.

When it comes to optimizing your pricing strategy, your goal is to 'get more' from 'the same'...

Regular Pricing Strategy   Optimized Pricing Strategy

The following are some product pricing strategies that help you *get more* from *the same*, to maximize your profits...

Adjust Your Pricing to New Market Realities

Your previous pricing strategies were grounded in assumptions about your products'...

| Market Size | + | Level of Competition | + | Consumer Demand |

COVID will have fundamentally shifted many of these assumptions. Your industry may have shrunk, competitors may have lowered their prices, and customer wallets may have become a little tighter.

Your products' prices should not be a static case of set-and-forget—they need to reflect the market realities you operate within.

Ensure you revisit many of the assumptions that underscore your products' prices and update them if and when appropriate.

Communicate Your Value

With more competitive market conditions, there's a chance that your industry is experiencing a pricing 'race-to-the-bottom'. This is disadvantageous to all businesses and leads to commoditized perceptions of the products and services you sell. In this environment, you and your competitors end up competing on *price*, regardless of appropriate margins or the value you actually provide.

To stand out in this environment, your business needs a point of differentiation. This should revolve around some superior value your customers will derive in selecting *your* product over your competitors'. Examples include…

Convenience		Features	
Customer Service		Performance	
Customization		Prestige	
Durability		Safety	
Efficiency		Sustainability	
Entertainment		Usability	
Functionality		Warranties	

What value drivers shape customer preferences these days? Do any have heightened significance in post-COVID times?... Make sure that any prioritized value drivers are communicated in your marketing.

Get Customers Hooked

As was just noted, you'll want to move away from starting the customer conversation with *price*. Unless you're positioning your business for ownership of the 'cheap and cheerful' market segment, of all your value drivers, prioritize others above price.

An effective tactic to achieve this is to enable customers to experience your products and appreciate their value first-hand. Once they've done this, making future purchases is less about taking a leap-of-faith, and more about continuing to derive the benefits they've come to enjoy.

In many instances, the markup between your product's production costs and the sale price to the customer can be substantial. Taking a cut on the initial purchase to secure a long tenure of relationship will likely justify the lost earnings. Consider also offering free trials, 'freemium' offerings and money-back guarantees to lower the barriers of initial resistance and hook customers in for the first of many purchases.

Calculate the Lifetime Value of Your Customers
It's easy to forget that you are not limited to only a 'cost-plus' pricing model. Using the cost-plus approach, you determine the price at which your products will be sold by simply adding your different costs with your desired profit margins...

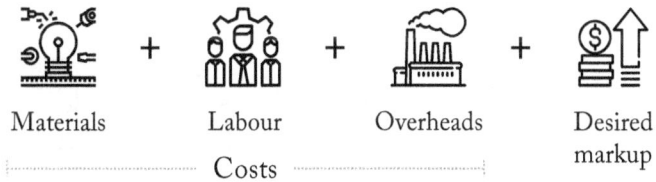

Materials + Labour + Overheads + Desired markup

Costs

Whilst neat and simple, this approach doesn't give due weight to the lifetime value of a repeat customer. A repeat customers' value may justify lowering prices to attract them initially, to then reap the rewards of a longstanding relationship resulting in multiple purchases...

Customer Lifetime Value = Average Sale Price X Average Number of Purchases

Balance any 'cost-plus' pricing approach with a nuanced consideration of the lifetime value you stand to gain from satisfied and loyal customers. Moving beyond a pure cost-plus approach necessitates supporting your pricing strategy with a good customer retention strategy that keeps customers sticky to your products. These loyal customers are the ones that will help you weather storms like COVID and other tough times in the future too.

Reduce Your Costs to Pass on Savings

If you wish to maintain your margins in the face of diminished sales and discounted prices, then your only available lever is to reduce your *costs*. Review your supply chain and see if there are opportunities for reducing your cost of goods sold in a way that doesn't materially impact the quality of your products.

Materials → Supplier → Factory → Distribution → Retailer → Customer

Explore new and innovative distribution channels that eliminate any of the overheads associated with getting your products into the hands of your customers. Instead of raising your prices to counter diminished sales volumes, consider trimming any less important product features that will enable you to cut costs.

Utilize Loss Leader Products

If you have a sizable product range with variance in margins across different product lines, you should consider using one of your higher-margin products as a 'loss-leader' for boosting customer engagement.

This is where one of your products is sold at a price *below* its market value to stimulate the sale of more profitable products within your product range. This tactic will be especially useful if you're trying to re-engage with existing customers, have experienced a reduction in customer purchase volumes, or seeking to attract new customers.

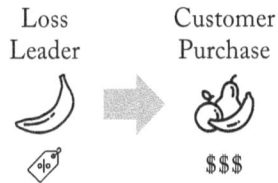

Loss Leader → Customer Purchase

$$$

Bundle Offerings for Additional Value

Bundled offerings serve a dual purpose. First and foremost, they provide additional value to your customers: a five-dollar combo meal comprising a burger, fries and soda is better value than buying a three-dollar burger plus two-dollar fries and a one-dollar soda separately...

$5   VS. $3   + $2   + $1

However, bundled offerings also help *you* sell more, since customers are incentivized to consider buying additional products they may not previously have purchased. During post-COVID times, when purse strings are tight, bundled offerings represent value-for-money in the eyes of price-conscious customers.

Take advantage of specific products with higher margins and lower costs, or inventory that you've earmarked for immediate clearance.

Offer Installment Payment Plans

For many businesses, a reduction in sales may not be reflective of a depreciated appetite for your products or services. It may just be a symptom of customers simply having less cash. There's a good chance that your prices remain fair and customer interest still remains high—as may likely be the case in these post-COVID times.

Remove cash flow roadblocks by making it as easy as possible for your customers to pay. Three installments of one hundred dollars over three months is easier to digest than one upfront payment of three hundred dollars...

The 'Buy Now Pay Later' model has become popular in recent times. Evidence suggests that it promotes consumer purchasing and additional spend. When times are tough, these flexible payment options may represent the difference between customers buying or not.

Provide Discounts for Cash and Early Payments

The flip side of this is offering discounts for paying upfront and/or with cash.

VS.

In the customer's eyes, the baseline value of the product remains, however now with the additional value of a discount.

Create Tiered Pricing Across Your Product Mix

Not all products are created equal. Different products with different costs are sold to different customers in different markets. All of these variables should impact your product pricing strategy.

Having a one-size-fits-all approach to product pricing will inevitably result in over or under-charging your customers. Map out your product mix and create a granular pricing strategy that leverages key differences amongst the different things you sell...

	Product □	Product ○	Product △
Costs	$	$$	$$$
Customer			
Competition	Medium	High	Low
Price	$$	$	$$$

Make sure that this strategy reflects contemporary changes to your costs, customer and competition resulting from COVID.

Re-Build Your Brand

COVID was first and foremost a health crisis of immense magnitude. It also led to an existential crisis for many small businesses—in the face of dissipating industries, disappearing customers and diminished access to supplies; businesses were left pondering... *am I still even relevant?*

Sadly, for some businesses, the impacts of COVID were the nail in the coffin that made resuscitation impossible. However, for the vast majority of businesses, this crisis represents a new dawn and opportunity for rejuvenation.

Who your business is at its core is best exemplified through your *brand*. And despite being widely accepted as a critical component of business success, branding remains an often-misunderstood concept.

At its most basic level, your brand is the sum of several key elements. These elements include your...

Identity + Perception + Personality + Positioning + Promise + Purpose + Values

Use this time as an opportunity to 're-imagine' who you are and want to be. Combine this with your rigorous market research and solid grasp of your target customers' needs and wants. Your brand then becomes a function of who you want to be, fused with who your customers want you to be too.

Your brand is critical as it cascades through every element of the products you sell and how your offerings are received by the market.

Current times provide you with an opportunity to go back to the drawing board and re-base your brand. When customers think about your business, how do you want them to feel? What reactions do you want them to have?

Instead of thinking about how you're able to *recreate* the business you once were, ask yourself what kind of business you'd *like to be*—these may be two very different things. And that's a good thing... Businesses evolve. Expectations change. Realities morph. Now is the time to get on the front-foot and re-build your brand.

So, how do you actually go about re-building your brand?

Determine Your Reason for Being

Be clear on your *purpose*. Knowing where you're trying to go will eliminate many of the obstacles that are stopping you from getting there. If you communicate your purpose with customers and your team, you'll win advocates that make the journey to realizing your goals not only faster, but a more enjoyable one too.

Decide What Makes You, *You*

Customers have become more discerning than ever. They have individual wants and needs, and are tired of uninspiring cookie-cutter product offerings. Don't shy away from standing out from the crowd. Carving out a niche will help with competitive differentiation.

In the aftermath of COVID, the future looks greatly different to the past, and customers are looking for captains to lead that journey—wear your unique identity as a badge of honor.

79

Figure Out Your Most Important Values

Different brands value different things. There is no objective *right* or *wrong* when it comes to values. Part of being authentic is living the values that matter most to you. Brainstorm a shortlist of the values that are most important to your business...

Accountability		Humility	
Balance		Idealism	
Boldness		Improvement	
Communication		Innovation	
Community		Integrity	
Compliance		Leadership	
Courage		Learning	
Dedication		Ownership	
Discipline		Partnership	
Diversity		Passion	
Environment		Quality	
Ethics		Results	
Fairness		Simplicity	
Fun		Teamwork	
Honesty		Trust	

Cull your shortlist down to the key values you hold dearest and want to be associated with. These are the values you intend your business to live and breathe each and every day.

In the fog of COVID, becoming an exemplar of your values will be an anchor of comfort for customers looking for reliable surety from the businesses they choose to deal with.

Consider How You Want to be Regarded

How you are perceived by customers is a critical determinant of their desire to purchase from you. Even if you address their pain points, few customers want to deal with a brand that is perceived negatively.

When supported with quality products and a renowned reputation, being the 'good guy' of your industry will create an unimpeded route to sales.

Can you think of any businesses that were well-regarded for the decisions they made throughout the COVID crisis? What lessons could be learnt going forwards for replicating similar perceptions?

Crystalize the Things Your Customers Expect From You

Your customers are looking for brands that not only *talk the talk*, but also *walk the walk*. Gimmicky or over-stated claims will be regarded as off-putting and be spotted from a mile away.

When it comes to making promises to your customers, under-promise and over-deliver. Create a customer experience that is enjoyable, reliable and that exceeds expectations.

Carve Out Your Coveted Place in the Market

Good branding involves positioning yourself exactly where you want to sit in the market. When your customers think of your brand, how do you want them to think about you vis-à-vis your competition?

Your Brand Positioning

Customer's Wants

Your Offering

Competition's Offering

Getting this right means knowing your customers and ensuring that the space you carve out is *relevant* and *genuine*.

Be Authentic

The impacts of COVID have left many customers with 'consumer scar tissue'. They're ready to move forward, but the aftermath of recent experiences are far from forgotten. Customers are looking for businesses they can genuinely trust. They are looking for businesses that behave beyond buzzwords. Become one of those businesses.

Appreciate That Branding is a Team Effort

To achieve true authenticity, your brand needs to permeate through everything that you do, and be lived by everyone that does it. As should be obvious by now, your brand is so much more than just your logo.

It is the level of support you provide to your customers. It is the language you use when you answer the phone. It is the clothes that are worn to the workplace. All of these require the efforts of your *entire* team.

Make sure that your team are involved in re-building your brand. Their perspectives and input should be valued and incorporated. *You* may own your business, but your *business* owns your brand.

Run a Disciplined Process to Re-Build the Brand

Understanding what's involved in building a brand is one thing, but this needs to come to life by running a disciplined process...

1. *Research*

Start by understanding your customers and their current perceptions of *yours* and your *competitors'* brand.

2. *Define*

Define your future-state brand, develop a roll-out plan and ensure you have all supporting collateral necessary for its delivery.

3. *Deliver*

Allow your brand to come to life, remembering that delivering your brand is not a moment-in-time event.

4. *Optimize*

Measure and track your results, as well as hypothesize and test continuous improvement opportunities; implementing the ones that work.

Put Your Personality on Display

Now more than ever, businesses are engaging in two-way dialogue with their customers. Top-down, one-way marketing messages make up an increasingly smaller share of marketing communications.

Your brand needs to infuse every facet of the *voice* with which you speak. This includes your:

- Branding guidelines
- Color palette
- Images
- Language
- Logos
- Marketing
- Messaging
- Packaging
- Promo material
- Typography
- Uniforms
- Website

Whilst COVID may have been the crisis nobody asked for, use it as the defining moment for when your business put its renewed personality back out on display.

Improve Your Offering With Better Customer Feedback

Prior to COVID, some businesses could be accused of having taken their customers' opinions for granted. These businesses weren't necessarily rude or dismissive—they simply operated on 'cruise control'—satisfying the business that came its way, without too much consideration for the actual opinions or perspectives of customers.

This all changed with the impacts of COVID, which disrupted many traditional buyer-seller power dynamics: demand dried up; customers spent less; seller competition became fiercer. For many businesses, it put the ball back in the court of the *customer.*

Now more than ever, businesses are in no position to take their customers' opinions and perspectives for granted. It was important before. It is extra important now.

Beyond these new power dynamics, gaining customer feedback is helpful for...

- Addressing product faults
- Building customer relationships
- Establishing your brand
- Gaining external perspectives
- Improving business processes
- Increasing customer retention
- Informing strategic decisions
- Optimizing customer experiences
- Quantifying customer satisfaction
- Resolving problems quicker

All of these outcomes help you improve your product offerings.

So, how do you go about getting better customer feedback?

Monitor Feedback on Digital Channels

Have you ever done a Google search on your own business? You may be surprised at what comes up! Your online reputation might reveal a wealth of insights on what customers truly think about your business and its products.

This may be as explicit as an opinion expressed on a consumer review website, or as subtle as a mention on a social media post. They may be compliments, or they may be criticisms.

Either way, these hidden gems provide unfiltered perspectives from real-life customers that you're able to use to gain customer feedback and improve your offerings.

Talk to Your Customers

It should come as no great surprise to hear that it's important to talk to your customers. Talking to customers bridges the gulf between what you *assume* customers think, and what customers *actually* think.

The current times we're in may make this gulf greater than ever before…

Pre-COVID	Post-COVID
Customer's Reality	
	Customer's Reality
Your Assumptions	
	Your Assumptions

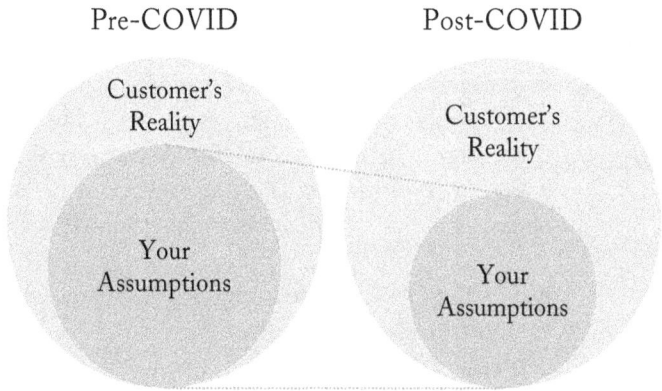

The impacts of COVID mean that for many customers, their consumer habits and buying drivers have shifted. It is imperative that you remain on top of new customer realities to be able to improve your offering based on the feedback that you hear.

When talking to your customers, make sure to...

- Acknowledge the uniqueness of each perspective
- Be opportunistic in gaining chances to talk
- Discuss whatever the customer is willing to share
- Maximize the frequency of touchpoint moments
- Have conversations with *groups* and *individuals*
- Involve team members from all business functions
- Leverage your social media presence for access
- Preference face-to-face interactions where possible
- Speak with both *existing* and *target* customers
- Value hearing both the *good* and the *bad*

Specifically Contact Past Customers

The speed of modern-day life and business often deprive us of the good old-fashioned conversations we used to have with customers in times gone by. However, these conversations remain one of the most powerful means by which a business is able to obtain rich and honest perspectives on what their customers truly think about them.

Since they're past customers, the business is assured that feedback reflects the opinions of those that have actually interacted with their products.

Use these novel times as an excuse for reconnecting and checking-in with past customers. Your efforts to do so and interest in their perspectives should make it easier to find obliging volunteers.

Speak With Key Team Members

Some of your employees operate at the coalface of your business and interact with customers more frequently than others. Your salespeople, for example, might be having daily conversations with customers—hearing about their pain points and experiences with yours and your competitors' offerings.

These team members act as proxy mouthpieces for your customers. They are able to provide insights into what customers like and dislike, and how you're able to improve your offerings.

Request Immediate Feedback After Purchase

Timing is important—asking customers to share their thoughts straight after purchase will provide unique perspectives that shed light on a wealth of key product insights. This moment represents the customer's arrival at the bottom of your sales funnel and the completion of their buying cycle.

There's a good chance they've considered purchasing from your competitors, so the insights you gain may prove helpful in understanding the rest of the market too.

Even though they purchased, the experience may not have been seamless. You might receive feedback that illuminates opportunities for improving your processes, in addition to ways of improving the actual offering itself.

Conduct Surveys

Surveys allow you to ask targeted questions that help fill the blanks around your products and services. They can be both qualitative and quantitative, and enable you to gain both macro and micro perspectives. These insights help build a holistic snapshot of consumer sentiment on topics of interest to you and the business.

Critical success factors include the survey design, asking the right questions and obtaining a sufficient sample size from which you're able to draw meaningful conclusions. To improve your offerings, use surveys to measure things like…

- Brand perceptions
- Customer effort
- Customer experience
- Customer loyalty
- Customer satisfaction
- Product perceptions

Gain Feedback With Incentives

Customers that voluntarily provide feedback typically fall into one of two camps...

Advocates
with strong views in *favor* of your offerings

Critics
with strong views that are *not in favor* of your offerings

This is because the motivation to share feedback will be fervid when it is attached to a strongly-held view...

To address this conundrum, offer customers an incentive to provide feedback; like a small gift, discount or access to special promotions.

Tap Visitors to Your Website

Whether you sell products online, or simply share basic information, almost all businesses these days have a website (and if you don't, you should!).

Visitors to your site aren't just random individuals—they are potential customers coming to either learn more about who you are, understand more about what you offer, or most desirably, make a purchase.

In short, one way or another, they are *exactly* the type of people you want to be gaining customer feedback from.

Add features to your website that elevate it into a bi-directional communication tool that both *shares* and *collects* information. Examples of customer feedback features you're able to add include...

- 'Artificial Intelligence' chatbots
- 'Exit intent' popups
- Feedback buttons
- Live chat
- Net Promoter Score popups
- Post-purchase surveys

Review Your Web Analytics

Your website's analytics provide a goldmine of insights that allow you to draw inferences around customer perspectives and perceptions. Who's coming to visit? What pages are they looking at? How long do they spend looking at which pages? These are just some of the questions you're able to answer by reviewing your web analytics...

www.company.com/product-abc	www.company.com/product-xyz
100 visitors	500 visitors
01:15 on page	03:45 on page
90% Bounce Rate	40% Bounce Rate

A product page with a low bounce rate, for example, may indicate greater interest in a product than a similar product page with a high bounce rate. This should trigger further investigations between the two offerings, that might explain these underlying differences.

In addition to web analytics, you're also able to add software that runs in the background and records your visitors' sessions as 'heatmaps' that show you how visitors are interacting with your website.

Use all of these tools to make inferences on ways to improve your customer offerings, starting with your website marketing effort.

Simply Watch and Observe

When was the last time you just blended in with the background and watched customers do their thing? It's not scientific, but just watching real-life customers interact with your business helps keep a healthy finger on the pulse of customer action and intent.

Now more than ever, you'll want to see first-hand how customers are behaving. Make sure you set time aside every now and then to just observe real-life customers make real-world interactions with your business.

Cost-Effectively Differentiate Yourself on Quality

With lower demand and diminishing margins, now more than ever you need a *point of differentiation* to stand out from the competition.

There are no shortage of levers you're able to pull to differentiate your business: you could customize your offering; you could add additional features; you could make your products more durable... the possibilities are endless.

At the end of the day, *your* knowledge of *your* business and *your* customers, market and products; should inform which differentiating levers *you* decide to pull.

However, a time-tested differential that's near universally-relevant for these challenging circumstances is a focus on lifting the quality standards of your products. But what actually is product *quality*?

It's the degree to which your products are perceived as meeting (and exceeding) the customer's expectations.

Put yourself in the shoes of a customer deciding which product they wish to buy. They're confronted with three options...

	Option 1 Low Quality	*Option 2* Regular Quality	*Option 3* High Quality
Pre-COVID:	$$	$$$	$$$$$
Post-COVID:	$	$$	$$$

Decreased demand as a result of COVID may have led to a reduction of prices. Suddenly, the price differentials between high-quality products and all other alternatives have become smaller.

Quality may take on a multitude of subjective characteristics. Ensure you understand your customers' expectations, to present them with products they won't be disappointed to purchase. When done right, higher quality does not necessitate higher costs or premium pricing.

So, how do you go about cost-effectively differentiating yourself on *quality*?

Get on the Front-Foot With Customer-Centricity

To differentiate yourself on quality, you first need to become a quality-focused business. Because of subjectivity on what that actually means, it requires first understanding what *quality* means to your customer.

Customer-centricity is quality's big brother. Without putting your customer at the centre of your quality-enhancing endeavours, you'll have limited success in raising the bar of your business' quality standards.

Integrate Quality Into Your Business' Culture and Training

Differentiating yourself on quality cannot be an afterthought and is not something that's just retrofitted to products. It demands a proactive effort that begins long before offerings end up in the hands of your customers, and manifests itself across all functions of your business.

Part of creating a business-wide focus on quality is integrating that focus into your day-to-day modus operandi. It needs to be lived and breathed by every one of your team members.

Quality standards won't just happen by accident. Structured learning interventions, like training courses and onboarding programs, will be essential. These should be supported on an ongoing basis by you and fellow leaders within your business.

Set Measurable Standards and Benchmarks

One of the challenges of differentiating yourself on quality is the subjective nature of what quality means to different people—in particular, your customers. You need to understand what expectations they have of your products, and set benchmarks that line up to those expectations.

Use the *SMART framework* to wrap goals around the quality standards you wish to achieve. Make sure that your goals are...

Specific	Measurable	Attainable	Relevant	Time-bound

Your industry may also already have recognized benchmarking standards, such as the *International Organization for Standardization (ISO)*, reflecting the level of quality you should be working towards.

Develop a Quality Management System

A Quality Management System (QMS) is a formal system that documents your policies, processes and procedures for maintaining and improving quality control. It includes things like:

- Continuous Improvement
- Manuals
- Measurement Tools
- Objectives
- Processes
- Record Keeping
- Roles and Responsibilities
- Satisfaction Monitoring

Your QMS serves as the go-to destination for anything and everything that has to do with quality. In introducing a QMS, you create a home for finding answers to any quality-related questions and eliminate ambiguity around what quality means for the business and your team.

Familiarize Yourself With Your Products

It's difficult to maintain high standards of product quality if you aren't first familiar with your products yourself. Don't leave it to your customers to alert you about your products' shortcomings.

Customer complaints should be incidental to your proactive efforts to create the highest quality products. This starts with preventing issues long before the customer ever has a chance to identify them themselves.

As a result of COVID, certain products will have new quality standard expectations associated with them. Examples include products emanating from the retail, food, travel, hospitality and cleaning industries. If your business works within this space, familiarity with your products, and embedding quality standards, becomes a non-negotiable.

Especially during these times, getting ahead of the curve on quality can create significant competitive advantages.

Test Products and Get Feedback From Real Customers

An exception to the principle of never placing inferior products into the hands of customers is *product testing*. This is the activity of giving 'beta' products to real customers for the specific purpose of understanding how the product can be improved.

Products may therefore be of a lower quality standard than would otherwise be acceptable if released for general public consumption.

Through beta testing, you're able to simulate the feedback you'd receive in the real-world, without the consequences to your brand or reputation.

Before embarking on product testing, iron out as many quality issues as you're able to identify and anticipate— beta testing should not become a convenient alternative to incomplete product development.

Personally Inspect Your Key Product Processes

It's easy for 'quality' to exist as just a theoretical concept that lives nowhere but on paper. *Your* goal is to bake it into the DNA of every element of your entire business. Take time out to observe your key product processes; like production, distribution and customer service.

You'll likely spot issues in need of remediation and opportunities for immediate improvement. These shortcomings are often just legacy issues and are easily fixable, so becoming proactive in identifying them is often half the job done already.

Improve Quality via Customer Issues and Complaints

Despite your best endeavours to place quality on a pedestal, issues will inevitably still occur from time to time. It's critical to get on top of these as quickly as possible. Customer complaints can—in this context— help you do just that.

Becoming aware of these issues is by no means a bad thing—even if it took a customer complaint to make you aware of it. They demonstrate that you're the kind of business that embraces customer feedback and that you have effective continuous improvement processes. That logic rings true so long as you rectify the issue as quickly as possible upon becoming aware of it. This invariably creates a continuous cycle of product improvements...

When you embrace customer issues and complaints in the spirit of *improvement*, you become a business that's set-up to succeed in differentiating itself on quality.

Deploy Technology and Upgrades to Uphold Quality Standards

Ask yourself the question: *is it time to upgrade my production instruments?* Whether you are a product or service-based business, *quality* often hinges on the tools and technologies used to produce and deploy your offerings.

You may have excellent processes but outdated technologies, which may be responsible for inadvertently lowering your quality standards.

There are often big expenses involved in upgrading technology. It's understandable that any uptick in quality needs to be balanced against the costs involved in getting there. COVID-related cost-controls may make immediate upgrades of technologies unfeasible.

Nonetheless, consider this option regardless of where you end up landing, and remain mindful of upgrades for when more favorable circumstances may allow them.

Review Results and Make Continuous Improvements

It's difficult to improve your quality standards if you don't know where they're currently at. You therefore need to benchmark and measure your effectiveness at maintaining quality standards using various evidence-based quantitative methods.

For example, the following quality-related metrics may be useful for benchmarking and measuring...

- Customer loyalty and retention
- Customer returns and complaints
- Levels of customer (dis)satisfaction
- Production fault rates

Employ the Japanese *Kaizen* principle of continuous improvement that translates these inputs into organisation-wide embedded improvements.

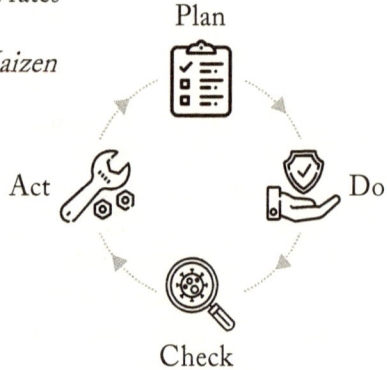

Plan

Do

Check

Act

Case Study: Product

Context

Tony runs a small independent toy shop.

When COVID hit, the business shut down for three months. In addition to one quarter of his annual revenue disappearing, customers have been slow to return even after his doors reopened.

This represents a shock for Tony, as the business had operated successfully for the past 25 years.

Tony now worries whether customers will continue to make the discretionary purchase of toys in the future. He is also unsure how he is able to lure customers back into the store and get back some of his old groove.

Actions

Tony used the time in 'lockdown' to get in touch with some of his longstanding customers to better understand the things about his business that they do and don't like.

He is happy to hear mostly glowing reviews, but is fascinated to learn that many are disappointed by the limited product range he stocks.

Tony decides to add video games and puzzles as new product lines to address their frustrations.

Tony identified products with healthy margins in leading product categories, and earmarked some as 'loss leader' products.

He also signed-up with a Buy Now Pay Later financier company so that he's able to offer installment payment plans for his more expensive products.

He recognizes that his products bring lots of joy and happiness to people—things that customers were craving in the wake of COVID. He therefore updates his branding and marketing to reflect this.

Tony also makes a personal commitment to better acquaint himself with all of his products to ensure that they meet the highest quality standards that customers expect. Quality too, becomes integral to his brand.

Results

The video games and puzzle product lines now account for 35% of revenue.

They have also attracted lots of new customers, and have allowed him to discontinue a number of less-profitable products.

Many of these new customers are younger, and love the installment payment plans he now offers. Average purchases for those that use these plans are double the average of those that don't.

Since implementing new quality controls, product returns have halved.

Growth

Go Deeper and Broader in New and Current Markets

Win New Customers Through Referrals

Increase Share of Wallet Through Cross-Selling and Upselling

Optimize Your Website to Win, Grow and Retain Customers

Growth Through Partnerships and Strategic Alliances

Go Deeper and Broader in New and Current Markets

COVID may be responsible for having placed your aspirational growth plans on ice for the time being. With pressures on finances, efforts to minimize risk, and not wishing to venture too far into unfamiliar territory; you may be bunkering down in 'safety' mode for the time being.

However, the impacts of COVID likely left a dent on your business' performance—sales may have declined, costs may have gone up, and profits may have shrunk. You may be turning your attention towards supplementary markets that have the potential to provide compensatory sources of revenue for your business.

COVID disrupted many 'traditional' market dynamics and created new opportunities that didn't previously exist (or which were previously much harder). Failure to consider new market opportunities may result in missing out on lucrative and practical opportunities for your business.

When it comes to tapping new markets, there are a number of options at your disposal. You could...

- Go deeper with existing products in markets currently served
- Take those same products to new markets
- Introduce new products within your current markets
- Create totally new products for totally new markets

This is best summarized by the *Ansoff matrix* framework:

	Existing Products	New Products
Existing Markets	Market Penetration	Product Development
New Markets	Market Development	Diversification

Increased risk

Each option represents unique opportunities and poses differing challenges and levels of risk. It's not always a clear-cut case of selecting *one* strategy over another, as there's some degree of overlap between approaches (for example, when are you entering a new market versus penetrating an untapped subset of a market you currently service?).

If you are considering taking your products to new or existing markets, make sure to consider the following things...

Fix Your 'Leaking Bucket'

A leaky bucket has two fixes: add more water or plug the leak. Before turning your attention to growth opportunities emanating from new markets, consider whether the same objectives could be met by 'plugging the leaks' of your existing customer bucket.

There are significant costs involved in acquiring a new customer—you'll spend big sums on the marketing required to move customers all the way from the top of the sales funnel down to the bottom.

In contrast, the costs of selling to existing customers is much lower. Repeat customers come with lower acquisition costs, spend more than one-off customers and possess greater lifetime value to your business. Since they're already familiar with your product, you spend less time conveying value and explaining features and benefits.

	New Customer	Existing Customer
Customer Acquisition Costs:	$$	$
Average Spend:	$	$$

Consider some of these customer retention strategies:

- 'Abandoned cart' and Thank You eCommerce emails
- Activate a customer communications calendar
- Build your email lists
- Develop customer loyalty programs
- Introduce a customer education and success program

Determine the Markets With Room to Grow

Whether it's deeper penetration of current markets, or looking for new customers in new markets, start by understanding just how big the size of the prize actually is. For both current and target markets, consider this from three different perspectives...

- *Total Addressable Market (TAM)*
  The value of the entire market

- *Serviceable Addressable Market (SAM)*
  The portion of the Total Addressable Market your business can actually service

- *Share Of Market (SOM)*
  The portion of the Serviceable Addressable Market that you can realistically capture

Ensure that whatever market growth strategy you run with, that the realistic Share Of Market that you expect to be able to capture translates into a sufficient reward to justify your efforts.

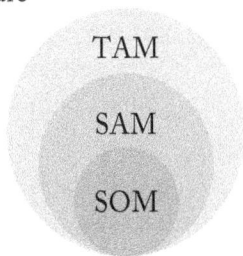

TAM

SAM

SOM

Conduct Rigorous Market Research

Whether pursuing a larger piece of the pie, or looking for 'new pies' all together, any of these goals will inevitably come at the expense of diminishing your competitors' market share. Conduct a competitive analysis of any market you're contemplating, to understand who's-who-in-the-zoo and gain a perspective on the lay of the land.

If you're considering entering *new markets*, the allure of gaining access to a new base of customers masks the hurdles that must first be overcome if you are to succeed.

Before diving head-first into a new market, use the *Porter's Five Forces* framework to assess the competitive environment of the market you're considering entering. Ask yourself questions around the following five key considerations:

- Threat of *new entrants*
- Threat of *substitutes*
- Bargaining power of *buyers*
- Bargaining power of *suppliers*
- Competitive *rivalry*

Once you've determined the competitive landscape of the target market, make sure to assess the macro-environmental factors of those markets too. A useful framework for doing this is conducting a *PESTLE Analysis*, that considers each of the following factors:

- Political
- Economic
- Social
- Technological
- Legal
- Environmental

Understand New Target Customer Profiles

You're able to rely on experience in understanding 'the customer' for markets you currently serve. However, when entering a new market, your ability to rely on this same intuition is diminished. Take rigorous measures to familiarize yourself with customer profiles in the new target market (like developing buyer personas) to inform relevant go-to-market strategies for the new market.

Also examine what the competition within the target market are currently doing. Understand their marketing to get a feel for the customer profiles they're already trying to appeal to. Instead of trying to re-invent the wheel, incorporate as many of these insights as appropriate.

Your review of competitor activity may also reveal market gaps in appealing to unaddressed customer pain points. These too represent opportunities for taking a commanding position within the target market.

Ultimately, should you decide to take your products to a new market, you'll need to embed these understandings of target customer profiles into product and marketing tweaks of your existing products. For example, you may need to use alternate branding, different messaging or translated copy on product packaging. All of this should be built off the back of a solid understanding of the target customer.

Leverage Your Competitive Advantages
When devising growth strategies, leverage your existing competitive advantages to achieve your desired goals.

Maybe you can make products *better, quicker* or *cheaper?* Maybe you already have a solid brand and positive reputation in other markets? Maybe you have supplier relationships in favorable locations?... Whatever the advantage, make sure it gets used when establishing your market footprint.

Identify New Distribution Opportunities

Before pursuing new markets to gain access to new customers, consider whether that same goal could be achieved by identifying new distribution channels within the existing markets you currently serve.

Broaden your thinking around how you currently conceive of 'markets that you serve': how truly *homogeneous* is this market, or is it made up of distinct sub-market segments?

If, for example, you're in the business of selling *toys* to *retailers*, there may be different types of *toy retailers* that you may (or may not) be currently selling to: there may be *large general retailers*, *national toy retailers* and *boutique toy shops*. A basic understanding of your relative penetration of each may reveal some pragmatic growth opportunities.

In addition to sub-market segmentation, consider whether additional distribution channels might provide access to new sales opportunities...

Affiliates   Re-sellers

Agents   Retailers

Distributors   Wholesalers

Finding new distribution channels in existing markets for products you already make will spawn new opportunities without many of the costs, complications or risks associated with other growth strategies.

If you are considering taking your products to new markets, you'll again need to determine the distribution channels that will get your products into the hands of target customers. In some instances, this may be as simple as replicating the channels used in markets you currently service. However, even when distribution channels are the 'same', they may still require new distributor relationships to be established.

Make sure that you also have a risk mitigation strategy if entering a new market, as it will inevitably involve risk. There may be significant capital outlay required to set up production facilities, distribution outlets as well as new marketing costs. All of these expenses are precious dollars being diverted from current markets. An example of a new market mitigation tactic is executing a phased performance-based go-to-market plan.

Consider Your Product Mix

Different products will have different appeal in different markets. You therefore need to consider your product mix with great regard when deciding whether to pursue deeper penetration of existing markets or entering into new markets.

Instead of working with a one-size-fits-all mindset to *all* markets, develop a segmented product mix for each unique market (or market segment) you plan to pursue:

	Market 1	Market 2	Market 3
Product 1	✓	✗	✓
Product 2	✗	✓	✓
Product 3	✓	✓	✓

With a holistic understanding of your product mix across all current and intended markets, you'll be better positioned to make important decisions, like whether to expand or contract certain product lines and relevant marketing tactics to deploy.

Offer Pricing Incentives

Depending on your growth intentions, there are a range of levers you're able to pull to achieve different objectives. Regardless of whether you're looking to go deeper within existing markets, enter new markets, or introduce new products; offering pricing incentives is one lever that can be used to support your efforts to achieve any of these goals.

Offering pricing incentives may not be sustainable in the long-term, but represents an effective tactic for building awareness, customer stickiness and stealing market share in the short term.

If you've suffered a significant decline in sales volumes and you are struggling to cover your fixed costs (or they simply represent a much bigger proportion of your total costs than they should), then pricing incentives may also be a powerful way to stimulate sales to allow you to defray your fixed costs across a larger number of purchases.

Different products operate with different margins, so the feasibility and duration of pricing incentives should be determined on a case-by-case basis. These incentives should also align with your specific growth objectives and operating realities.

Identify Your Points of Differentiation

Before pursuing growth opportunities, pause and consider what's different about *your* offering to anything else currently available in the market.

Whether you're looking to go deeper in markets you're already in, or you are venturing into new markets altogether, you need to be able to answer the question: *what am I offering customers that's different to what they currently already have access to today?* In short, why should customers care?

There's no limit to the discriminating attributes able to contribute to your unique value proposition, but without having notable points of differentiation, there's a good chance that customers won't take notice.

Instead of playing a guessing game, speak to real (current and potential) customers to understand their pain points and thoughts on existing products available in the market. Leverage any relationships with existing customers and supplement those with customer interviews, surveys and focus groups that help get inside the heads of your customers to understand the feasibility of your market growth aspirations.

Evolve a Product

The idea of a 'new' product could be interpreted to mean a number of different things. How new does *new* need to be? The reality is that variants of existing products can represent 'new' products too.

The lines may be a little blurry between what's new versus simply updated, but when it comes to new products, the intention remains the same: create something that's seen as *fresh*, *original* or *different* within the market.

Remember that product development is often no mean feat. It can require significant research and development costs, changes to your production processes, marketing and sales investments, and new team capability requirements.

Whilst the fruits of success should justify everything it took to get there, make sure that you have the resources to deliver, without impacting your current operations either.

Do early and upfront customer testing by placing prototypes of your new product into the hands of real-life customers to get feedback early. Not only will you gain invaluable feedback to optimize your product for official roll-out, but it will also prevent you from going down costly and time-wasting dead-end paths that are unlikely to succeed.

Win New Customers Through Referrals

Think about all the marketing and sales tactics you employ to win new customers: advertising, maintaining a social media presence, direct mail, telemarketing, attendance at trade shows, blogging on your website, email marketing, public relations, sales meetings—the list could go on and on. And how much time and money does all of this cost you? Probably quite a bit too.

In contrast, referral sales originate from those outside of your business. Referrers become a de-facto extension of your sales and marketing arm, helping to spread the message on who you are, what you do, and why you're great.

In contrast to the uphill battle of repeatedly needing to demonstrate credibility to those unfamiliar to you, referred customers will be less inclined to keep their 'guard up' against those whom they already know. Customers are typically predisposed to trusting a referrer, thus eliminating a major barrier to purchase. Winning new business through customer referrals is truly the low-hanging fruit when it comes to customer acquisition.

In contrast to other marketing and sales tactics, leads from referrals tend to be better quality, convert more readily and are typically faster to close. They are almost always cheaper to acquire in marketing costs, and since they are more likely to become repeat customers, end up having a higher lifetime value to your business.

So, how do you go about winning new customers through referrals?

Establish a Formal Customer Referral Program

The natural starting point for seeking referrals is the introduction of a formal customer referral program. Instead of needing to go out and ask for referrals customer-to-customer, allow customers to proactively offer those same referrals of their own volition.

These customers are incentivized to do so by the receipt of some *reward*—most likely in the form of a freebie, special offer or discount.

Once these programs are established, make sure to let your customers know of their existence and what the benefits of participation will provide. If for no other reason, it's an additional touchpoint you gain with customers that shines a spotlight on the value that you offer.

Set Goals and Targets

Your ambition to win more sales as a result of referrals is likely to become dead in the water if it's not backed up with a solid plan that spells out *who*, *what*, *where*, *when* and *why*.

Set targets for how many referrals you would like, by when, and with whom. With foreknowledge of who you want to be referred to, you're able to 'work backward' and determine who within your network might be best positioned to connect you to those targets. All of this is much harder without clarity on referral goals and targets.

Make Referring Easy to Do

You will increase the chances of customers obliging to your requests for referrals by making their job as easy as possible. You'll also increase the chances of the referral being successful if you arm them with the best possible information to whet the appetite of those that are being referred.

Spell out exactly who you would like a referral to. This removes one less burden from the shoulders of the referrer.

Summarize a few bullet points about your business and the offering; making sure to give all key information to the referrer on a silver platter. It may also be useful to share select marketing resources like fact sheets or case studies that you have already created too.

Incentivize for Referrals

Different referrers will have different motivations for referring. In some instances, it will be because of an underlying positive relationship and desire to assist. At other times, the relationship might not be as strong, and lacks an organic impetus for selflessly wanting to help out.

For the latter, incentivize the referrer with a benefit they gain by making the referral. Clever referral gifting will share a benefit to *both* the giver and receiver of the referral—becoming a win-win for all.

For example, offer a discount that's applicable to both an existing and future (referred) customer if a referral is made and new business comes about as a result.

Time the Request

When is the best time to ask for a referral? After the explicit demonstration of value.

Very often, requests for referrals come at a time that goods are received or projects delivered. What else typically comes at this time? The *bill*. Naturally, you want to distance the referral request from anything that may sour a favorable disposition towards you.

Whilst there's not much you're able to do about charging your customers for the goods and services you provide, you can still choose when you're able to ask for the referral. Be strategic and pick opportune moments where the customer will have had a chance to personally appreciate the value that they've gained from you.

Give and Take

Giving referrals is all about sharing the love and paying it forward. You're asking others to do this for you, but there's nothing stopping you from doing it for others too.

Whether it's intended as a quid-pro-quo or simply as a gesture that recognizes value you've received from others, get in the habit of passing on referrals for other businesses. Doing this proactively will clear the decks for when it comes time to reaching out to others and asking them to return the favour.

Maintain Multiple Touchpoints With Those That are Referred

Not all referrals will bear immediate fruits. You may need multiple touchpoints to take things from the initial introduction to a sale, by warming them up over time. Schedule these touchpoints to ensure that they actually occur and don't fall through the cracks.

The last thing you want is to come across as annoying—this makes you look bad to the person being referred, and reflects poorly on the referee, to whom you'll want to express your gratitude. Make sure that any post-introductory follow-up respects these principles with the sensitivity and appropriateness that they require.

Make Sharing Your Content Easy

Referrals come in many shapes and sizes. We often think of referrals first and foremost as an explicit introduction of your business to another potential customer. This may be first prize, but there are other—more subtle—forms that a referral may also take, like a de facto endorsement represented by sharing your marketing assets.

There's a good chance that you already produce great marketing material that lives on the web. Make sure that these assets are easily sharable. Existing customers may wish to share things from great businesses they've worked with. Alternatively, strangers may stumble across things they believe could be of interest to others they know too.

Referrals may take the form of an email, direct message or social media post. Whichever way it is delivered, take advantage of how easily things are able to be shared online, to connect your business with those that may not have known about you before.

Prepare Yourself for New Customers

You should prepare specific marketing assets that explain your business to newly-referred customers. These help reduce barriers to conversion and makes a new customer's onboarding easier for both you and them.

In addition to incentives that converted them into customers in the first place, you may wish to provide new customers with a discount, freebie or benefit as thanks for having taken the 'leap of faith', and beginning the journey of building a fruitful long-term relationship.

Say Thank You

Following up to say *thank you* to referees will acknowledge their efforts in assisting, and leave the door open to requesting additional referrals in the future. Failure to recognize the time they've taken to help you will mean they're less likely to want to help out again in the future.

The reverse is also true: referees are more likely to continue referring you—maybe even proactively—when their assistance is met with the appreciation and recognition it rightfully deserves.

Increase Share of Wallet Through Cross-Selling and Upselling

If we go back to our TAM-SAM-SOM framework from before, we understand that that your Share of Market (SOM) is the proportion of the Serviceable Addressable Market (SAM) that you've managed to capture.

Your growth options aren't constrained to just considering new products or new markets. You can also grow by increasing your market share within the existing markets you currently service without the need to create new products. This is known as market penetration and your goal here is to increase your share of market...

FROM   TO

Total
Addressable Market

Serviceable
Addressable Market

Share of
Market

Two effective tactics for increasing market share are cross-selling and upselling. *Cross-selling* is the practice of selling additional products to customers. *Upselling* is the practice of enticing customers to purchase a more expensive item, upgrade or add-on.

Both tactics provide a number of benefits to both you and the customer:

- Improved customer experience
- Increased awareness of offerings
- Increased customer loyalty
- Increased revenue
- Increased value to customer
- Lower customer acquisition costs

Product:	🍔	🚗	📷	📱	⭕
Upsell:	🍔	🚙	📷	📱	💍
Cross-Sell:	🍟				👂

Following are some ways you're able to increase your share of wallet through cross-sells and upsells...

Determine Your Motivations

Aside from providing additional value for your customers, crystalize the specific motivations for upselling and cross-selling on your end. Are you trying to...

- Extract maximum revenue from each sale?
- Attract new customers?
- Clear old stock?
- Showcase new products?

Depending on what your goal(s) actually are, the strategies you use to achieve those objectives will differ.

Prioritize Upselling

Both upselling and cross-selling are effective strategies for adding additional customer value and helping you achieve other business goals, like increased sales. However, where possible, lead with *upselling* and follow with *cross-selling*.

Both opportunities exist only because the customer wishes to make an initial purchase. However, *upselling* aligns directly with the original product being purchased. Cross-selling, on the other hand, actually diverts their attention away from the initial product.

Upsell → *Cross-Sell* →

The last thing you want is to gamble away *any* purchase, at the expense of an *only potential* secondary purchase. Make sure that you sequence your strategies appropriately and intelligently.

Incentivize and Reward

In addition to incentivized pricing, you're also able to offer additional incentives and rewards to encourage the customer to accept your upsell and cross-sell recommendations. For example...

Customers that spend over $100 receive free shipping

or

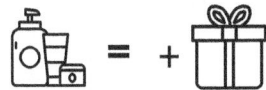

Customers that buy bundled offerings receive a free gift

Explain Not Just *What*, but *Why* You Recommend

Naturally, the focus of your upsell and cross-sell strategies should be sharing relevant products or services that complement the original product that the customer wishes to purchase. However, your chances of success will increase greatly if you're able to explain not only *what* else you recommend they consider, but equally-importantly, *why* you recommend it too...

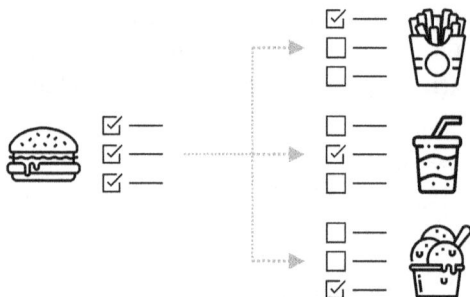

Let customers know about complimentary features and benefits derived from using both products in conjunction, or additional benefits gained from using a similar—but superior—product.

Time Your Recommendations

The success of your upsells and cross-sells will hinge largely on the timing of the offers. Your customers need to first and foremost feel comfortable with their initial primary purchase. Only then is it appropriate that they consider upgrades or complementary offerings.

You'll want to catch customers whilst they are still in a 'buying mood'. For example, if you have an eCommerce website, this would line up with your *Product*, *Checkout* or *Thank You* pages.

For cross-sell opportunities, it's often strategic to wait an appropriate amount of time to allow the customer to personally appreciate value from use of their original purchase. For example, send customers a follow-up cross-sell email a few weeks after their initial purchase...

Offer Encouraging Pricing

Use special pricing to incentivize customers to consider additional or more expensive products.

For service offerings, you can offer *trial pricing* to lower the barriers of resistance to any of your upsell or cross-sell offers. With trial pricing, you're essentially suggesting that customers have little to lose, by providing the opportunity to sample the offering without any commitment to purchase.

Alternatively, you can offer *bundle pricing*. This utilizes your knowledge that the customer has a specific product in mind, to encourage them to consider additional related products too. These additional products are incentivized with discount prices:

Buy phone...   *Get phone case for 50%*

Maintain Relevance in Your Marketing

Ensure that you maintain relevance in the marketing of your upsell and cross-sell strategies. Just because *you* want to push a particular product, doesn't mean that the customer wants to hear about it.

Understanding your different customer types will allow you to market them the right products wrapped in the right marketing messaging too. For example, a hairdresser that's buying professional hair products should be marketed to differently than an individual purchasing personal care hair products for themselves...

VS.

Maintaining relevance in your marketing will assist in communicating inherent value in your upsell and cross-sell recommendations.

Only Offer Relevant Recommendations

In addition to your marketing, your actual upsell and cross-sell product recommendations need to be appropriate too. Your recommendations should only be those that are relevant to the product the customer was originally interested in.

Similarly, the price points of these recommendations should be commensurate with the initial product too. There's no point trying to upsell a customer from a *Ford* to a *Ferrari.*

For example, if a customer purchases a camera, then a camera lens is an appropriate cross-sell. But if that lens costs twice as much as the camera itself, you may want to reconsider a more appropriate recommendation.

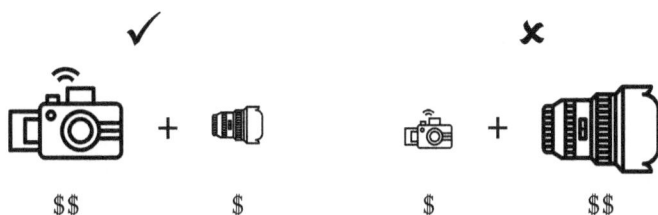

Start Doing Re-Marketing

In the digital space, there are plenty of opportunities to 're-market' to current and potential customers. Re-marketing is the practice of serving a targeted marketing message to someone that has been to your website or done something online that indicates some form of buying intent.

Once someone has visited your website, you're able to show them an advertisement on other websites and social media that promotes specific products or services you sell.

You're able to take this one step further and show specific people specific ads based on your knowledge of the pages they've visited on your site and the products you can confidently infer they have an interest in.

For example, if somebody checked out shoes on your website, let them know about other related products that may compliment shoes and potentially also be of interest to them. You can make this even more appealing by offering a special discount on these products if purchased straight away.

Help. Don't Hinder.

Remember that upsell and cross-sell opportunities only present themselves because the customer is interested in making an initial purchase with you.

There's therefore goodwill and trust already in the bank. This shouldn't be gambled with in the hope of making a bigger or better sale *if* you run the risk of losing *any* sale at all.

Fortunately, this needn't be an *either-or* decision. So long as you don't bombard the customer, and ensure that any upsell or cross-sell suggestions provide them with additional value, then your recommendations—whether embraced or not—should be well-received.

Optimize Your Website to Win, Grow and Retain Customers

It can be taken as a given that you already have a website, and that the benefits of having a website are likely already well-understood by you. However, the era of post-COVID recovery demands connecting like never before with your target customers, as well as doing so in cost-effective ways.

There is no greater impact you could make to your marketing efforts at lesser cost than *optimizing your website*. Why? Because your website is the centrepiece of all of your other marketing activities and investments. At the end of the day, almost everything reverts back to your website...

You might be doing a whole range of marketing activities across a broad spectrum of channels. Maybe you do Google Ads. Maybe you advertise on Facebook. Maybe you send a weekly company newsletter... Whatever you do, each of these marketing tactics aim to draw eyeballs to your website as one of—if not *the* most—important goals.

With this being the case, you need to think about your website as a 'virtual showroom' for your business, no different to a physical showroom that customers would come and visit.

What impression do you want customers to have when visiting your physical shopfront? What impression do you want customers to have when walking into your office? What impression should customers be left with after talking to your staff?

Whatever the answers are to those questions, so too should they equally apply to your website. In fact, having a website that leaves a bad taste in customers' mouths runs the risk of actually causing more harm than not having a website at all.

Given that it's the 21st century, and almost every customer expects the businesses they deal with to have a website, you don't have much of an option to do anything *but* to have a website that puts your best foot forward.

The good news is that creating a top-class website is relatively simple and inexpensive. Furthermore, this small investment enhances the return on investment you derive from your other marketing investments too. How so? Let's walk through an example customer journey...

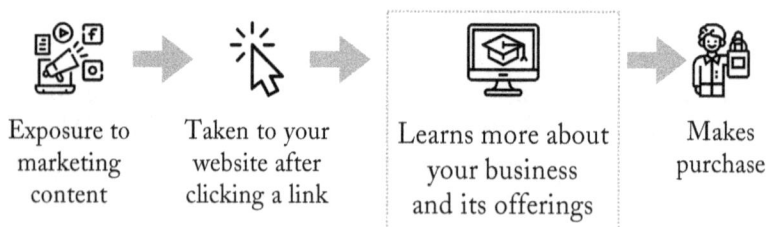

Exposure to marketing content	Taken to your website after clicking a link	Learns more about your business and its offerings	Makes purchase

Now, let's consider two marketing scenarios for a given year: one with a *poor* (✖) website, and one with a *great* (✔) website...

Marketing Tactic	Sales		Customer Acquisition Cost		Revenue		ROI	
	✖	✔	✖	✔	✖	✔	✖	✔
Google Ads $: 1,000 / 👆: 60	3	6	$333	$167	$3,000	$6,000	200%	500%
Social Media $: 750 / 👆: 40	2	4	$375	$188	$2,000	$4,000	167%	432%
Email Marketing $: 500/ 👆: 20	1	2	$500	$250	$1,000	$2,000	100%	300%
TOTALS $: 2,250 / 👆: 120	6	12	$375	$188	$6,000	$12,000	167%	432%

In our example, the difference between a great website and poor website translated into six additional sales worth $6,000 in revenue and representing an additional 265% return on marketing investment. It also decreased customer acquisition costs by 50%.

An additional benefit of optimizing your website is the ongoing value you derive the more time passes by. Development costs are diluted on an annualized basis, whilst concurrently delivering an increasing return on investment the longer the timeframe:

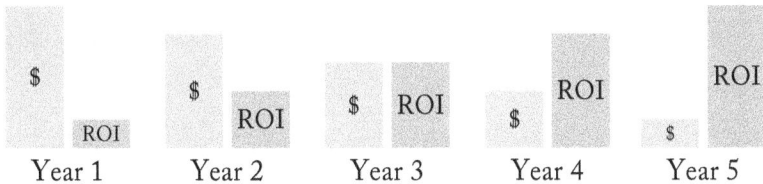

Year 1   Year 2   Year 3   Year 4   Year 5

This also compliments the greater return on investment you derive from all of the other marketing channels that direct customers to your website too.

These days it's relatively easy to find a cost-effective web developer able to build you a quality website for a good price. Your website isn't the place to be cutting corners if that short-term gain comes with long-term pain.

Depending on the complexity of your business and your appetite for building a best-of-breed site, there are always a number of *free* website builders you may wish to consider. Some of the more popular ones include:

WORDPRESS   WIX   weebly   SQUARESPACE   SITE123

When optimizing your website to win, grow and retain customers; here are a few things to keep in mind...

Keep it Simple, Clean and Professional

Your website is the online version of your bricks-and-mortar shopfront. In the same way that a physical outlet needs to be clean, well-branded and easy to navigate; so too does your website. You can't afford to leave a bad taste in prospective customers' mouths.

If the user experience is unenjoyable or overly-complicated, then the customer is able to look elsewhere with the click of a button.

Communicate Key Information

Having a website is like having a shop that's open 24/7—always accessible to customers whenever they want to visit. However, unlike a physical shop, it won't be manned by staff working every minute of every day.

This creates a responsibility to ensure you've done everything you can to provide all that a customer might want. Pre-empt their questions and ensure you share sufficient information around your business, your offering and value drivers of interest to customers.

Make Your Website Multi-Device Friendly

In the past, people used to access websites almost exclusively via their desktop computers. With the prevalence of smartphones and big data plans, more and more people are using their mobile and tablet devices just as much, if not more.

It is therefore in your interests to not only create a website that works well for desktop viewing, but equally so for mobile and tablet devices too. The mobile browsing experience is different to sitting in front of a computer with a big screen, so make sure the end-to-end user experience caters towards technological and browsing differences between devices.

Ensure that website load speeds are also optimized across all devices too.

Add Social Proof

Different people are looking for different things from your website. Depending on how close a customer is to making a purchase will determine what's required from you to get them over the line.

For customers far-advanced through their buying cycle, a major obstacle standing between where they are and making a purchase, is having faith in your business and its offering.

Social proof is the best way of providing this to them. It includes things like customer reviews and testimonials. Displaying these on your website validates past customer satisfaction in an authentic and believable way.

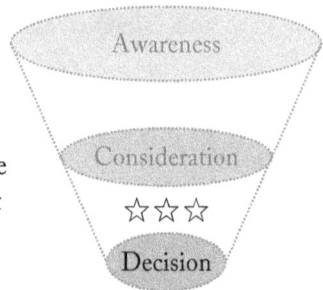

Ensure it's Easy to Get in Touch

Irrespective of what stage the customer is at in their buying cycle, you'll want to make it as easy as possible for them to get in touch for whatever reason they need to.

They may be looking for a certain product, trying to understand features and benefits, or may simply have a question that's not answered on your site. Whatever the reason, ensure that your website makes it as easy as possible for customers to get in touch.

Appreciate the difference between phone and email contact. There may be good reason you choose to exclusively display one over the other, but there's a certain level of confidence and customer service that comes with providing access to actually speaking with a real human via the phone.

Offer Incentives and Discounts

Through reviewing web analytics of the pages that get visited, you can infer things that are of probable interest to the visitors of your site. This allows you to offer incentives for things that are of likely interest too.

For example, if someone were looking at *running shoes* on your website, you may wish to display a 10% discount on all footwear products for the next 24 hours.

With minimal cost or complexity, you're able to add promotional features like customized popups that play to the visitor's interests and edge them closer towards making a purchase.

Share Great Content

Different customers will come to your website for different reasons depending on where they're at in their buying cycle. For some, they may just be looking for your contact details so they can make an immediate purchase. For others, they may be looking for general information that needn't necessarily have come specifically from you.

The extent to which you're able to convincingly prove your relevance will determine whether less-progressed visitors continue in the direction of a purchase with you. Consider adding a blog, tips and resources to serve as drawcards for coming to your website and giving prospective customers a sneak-peak of your capabilities and subject-matter expertise.

Incorporate Back Into Your Holistic Marketing Strategy

It's easy to think you've done your job once you've built a best-of-breed website. However, this will amount to little if no one ever visits it.

Creating your website is just the first step of the process. The next is deploying a multi-channel marketing strategy that magnetizes target customers towards it.

This involves deploying a suite of marketing tactics; like content marketing, Pay Per Click advertising and social media marketing.

Integrate your website into a holistic marketing strategy that leverages marketing automation and synchronizes with your other marketing channels like email and social media. Whilst your website naturally lends itself favorably to digital marketing tactics, don't forget to reference it in 'offline' marketing channels too—like direct mail and print advertisements.

With a holistic marketing strategy, you'll create a 'sticky' relationship with existing customers that promotes return visits to your website and encourages future purchases.

Review Your Web Analytics

With minimal effort and negligible costs, you're able to integrate web tracking and analytics software into your website. You gain access to customized reports that illuminate invaluable insights into...

- Who's vising your site
- What they're looking at
- Where they're coming from
- When they're using it
- Why they're visiting

All of this enables you to continually optimize your website to create high-impact targeted experiences that are appealing to visitors and support your sales efforts.

Add Live Chat

A hallmark characteristic of the modern digital consumer is their expectation of immediate service. Whether they're looking for information or wanting to make a purchase, visitors to your site don't like to wait. Live chat converts your website into a 24/7 resource able to assist customers with whatever it is that they need, and whenever it is they need it.

Live chat works *with* or *without* human intervention. It can answer questions, route customer inquiries and share customized messages to different people looking at different pages.

An 'Artificial Intelligence' live chatbot is a great addition to your website since all visitors are able to be 'warmed up', regardless of who they are or what initially brought them to your site.

Jane Doe X

Hello, how can I help you today?

I'm interested in your ABC product. Is it on special?

Yes it is. There is currently a 15% discount on that product!

Great. How do I order?

Click here, or share your contact details and I'll get someone to contact you asap.

Type ...

For example, you may wish to pre-program your chatbots with answers to frequently asked questions from customers that relate to COVID and your business.

Whilst it may seem like integrating Artificial Intelligence might be very difficult and/or expensive, a number of affordable and easy-to-integrate software tools make this task relatively straightforward. With a bit of foresight that pre-empts different visitor needs, you're able to use live chat to convert visitors into customers.

Growth Through Partnerships and Strategic Alliances

COVID may have forced your hand in pivoting the nature of your business' offerings. It may have required you to turn your attention to new markets. It may have necessitated adapting your product mix. These are just some of the many wholesale changes that may have been thrust upon you as a consequence of COVID.

Whilst many of these realities may have been triggered by forces outside your control, how you choose to respond to them *is not*. One response is the formation of partnerships and strategic alliances with other complimentary businesses.

There will be different motivations for entering into a partnership, though COVID may have elevated the relevance of considering doing so specifically *now...*

Your Business | Capabilities and Resources | Strategic Partner

Access to new customers | Economies of scale | Faster goal realization | Knowledge sharing | Sharing of risks and expenses

In addition to defusing competitive threats, a partnership may be an appropriate strategy for your business, its operating realities and any growth aspirations.

Despite the opportunity, they are not without their challenges. Since they involve working with partners *outside* of your business, there is an element of control that inevitably gets lost when embarking on the partnership.

The following are some key things to consider to maximize the utility and mitigate the risks of any partnership or strategic alliance you decide to pursue...

Recognize That It's Not an Alternative to Hiring

Make sure that you are entering into a partnership for the right reasons. A desire simply to recruit talent in the face of an inability to pay staffing costs is unlikely to be a legitimate reason alone.

You should look to partner with businesses that offer complementary capabilities, possess desirable resources or compensate for an internal weakness. Opportunities and threats that have resulted from COVID may elevate many of these considerations.

If your specific goal is to acquire talent or expand functional areas of the business, then consider funding options that can help you achieve that objective. Think long and hard before going down the path of a strategic alliance simply to circumvent needing to hire.

Determine Your Strengths and Weaknesses

The fundamental rationale for entering into a partnership is to overcome weaknesses within your business that are more easily solved through partnering than building those capabilities internally. Your partner should similarly be looking for complementary businesses whose strengths will overcome their own internal weaknesses.

Achieving this alignment can only take place once you've first done some introspection to identify your business' areas of greatest strength as well as internal weaknesses that are inhibiting your growth.

Identify Good Partners

You want to give your partnership every chance of succeeding, and setting yourself up for success begins with identifying who will be the best partner for you. Much like dating, you probably won't marry the first person you meet, so do your due diligence before diving head-first into a problematic partnership.

Having just determined your own strengths and weaknesses, and being clear on your strategic objectives; you'll be well-placed to identify potential candidates for good partners.

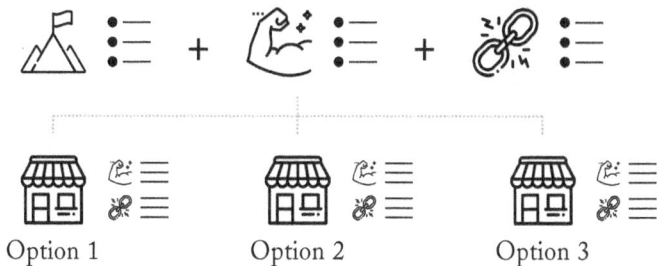

Option 1   Option 2   Option 3

141

Clarify the Purpose and Goals of the Partnership

Clarifying the purpose and goals of any partnership sets a flag on the hill for the strategic objectives that you and your partner are setting out to achieve. It explains the quid-pro-quo for why the two of you should be working together in the first place.

Clarifying the partnership's purpose makes clear that there's an opportunity to be realized, and that through mutual cooperation, those goals can be achieved.

Be Clear on Roles, Responsibilities and Accountabilities

Once you're aligned around your purpose and goals, it's time to translate these into an actual plan. You and your partner need to crystalize the specific roles and responsibilities each of you will be answerable for. In doing so, accountabilities are established upfront, which will prevent foreseeable issues down the track.

Intervene Early on Issues

It is important to extinguish issues as soon as they arise to prevent minor hitches escalating into major crises. Resolving issues in partnerships is a different kettle of fish to resolving issues in-house. When working in a partnership, different cultures, policies and procedures need to be reconciled.

Remain cognizant to sensitivities, over-communicate to eliminate ambiguities and be mindful of the overarching objective when working through any issues.

Always be Learning and Adapting

Even when entered into with rigorous due diligence, there are natural limits on being able to anticipate every partnership contingency that could possibly arise. Once it starts, you'll learn things that you'll wish you knew from the beginning.

The issue will not be in failing to identify these upfront—it will be in failing to internalize learnings and adapting them into the plan. The partnership will be stronger for having worked through new realities and integrating these learnings into the ongoing relationship.

Create a Relationship of Honesty

Just like personal relationships, the centrepiece of the partnership needs to be *honesty*. Having an honest relationship will drive trust and eliminate many of the distractions that stand between you and the goals you're both trying to achieve.

Needing to second-guess the motives of one another is an unnecessary waste of both yours and your partner's time, and prevents both from realizing mutual objectives via the path of least resistance.

Re-building your business in the wake of COVID represents a big enough challenge without needing to add unnecessary distractions that make the job harder than it need be.

Clarify How the Fruits of the Partnership Will be Distributed

It's important to take the partnership from something that's *theoretical* into something that's *practical*. This involves clarifying how the fruits of the partnership are going to be distributed between the two of you.

One of you may be allocating more in the form of your time and resources. It's important that these additional investments be recognized in the distribution of the partnership's financial outputs too. It's not always a case of 50/50, and if that's the situation for you, then call this out early and document it, for the sake of future reference.

Ensure You're Appropriately Legally Set-up

Similarly, make sure that you're legally structured and set-up to operate as a formal business partnership. It may seem like a logistical formality, but the consequences of not getting this right will be felt down the track.

Nip this foreseeable problem in the bud to allow you to focus on deriving unimpeded benefits of the partnership without complications.

Case Study: Growth

Context

Alan runs a local hardware shop.

When COVID hit, the shop was fortunate to be classified as an 'essential service', and allowed to remain open.

However, a general decrease in foot traffic and needing to compete with a large hardware retailer in the local area caused a reduction in sales. Sales had generally been decreasing since the large retailer entered the area two years ago, and Alan now worries that this pattern has been further entrenched by the impacts of COVID.

He now questions the likelihood of a turnaround, and the business' ongoing viability.

Actions

Alan conducts rigorous market research and identifies that despite having a strong market footprint with professional trade customers, there's a lot of room for growing his retail 'DIY' customer base. These customers are extra appreciative of the superior personal customer service that his business is able to provide.

Alan also introduces a delivery service for his larger professional trade customers.

The vast majority of Alan's customers are longstanding patrons that hold a favorable disposition towards his store.

Alan introduces a formal customer referral program that rewards customers with in-store credits to be redeemed on purchases. He runs a marketing campaign to let customers know about the program.

Alan also introduces a number of cross-sell promotions, and trains his team on upsell strategies and relevant products to be upsold.

He revamps his tired old website and starts with re-marketing ads on Google too.

Alan enters into a strategic partnership with the paint shop down the road, after realizing they both sell complementary offerings to similar customers.

Results

The partnership with the paint shop brings in no less than 30 new customers per week.

Alan's customer referral program also proves to be a big hit, and is now responsible for one-third of all new business. It has also resulted in existing customers coming back to use their store credits and make additional purchases.

Since introducing the cross-sell and upsell initiatives, product sales have risen by 20%, and the average purchase size grown by 25% too.

Operations

Update Your Business Plan to Reflect New Realities

Improve Your Processes to Achieve Efficiency Gains

Revise Your Organizational Structure for Smooth Operations

Make Meetings Matter

Improve Internal Communications to Recognize New Realities

Update Your Business Plan to Reflect New Realities

It may have been a while since you last sat down to formally review your business plan; or worse yet, you may not ever have done one at all. For better or worse, the COVID crisis is the trigger that necessitates doing so *now*.

If you have a business plan, it will likely maintain a lot of its original legitimacy. Unless your business is a fundamentally new beast; many, if not most of the sections, should retain much of its original currency.

However even parking COVID aside, your *business*, your *industry* and your *customers* would almost certainly all have evolved since creating any original plan. And when you *do* throw COVID into the mix, it becomes undeniable that things are simply different *now* to how they were *before*.

The purpose of a business plan is to demonstrate commercial feasibility, articulate business goals and create a roadmap for their attainment. It is intended to provide a 360° macro overview of the major components of your business, and serve as your North Star for making important business decisions that involve a diversity of stakeholders and timelines.

In the best of times, it is good practice to periodically re-visit your business plan and update it with new developments and information. In these post-COVID times, this becomes a non-negotiable.

Think about all the things that have been impacted by the virus, and your new operating reality...

Cash flow		Market dynamics
Competition		Marketing strategy
Customer behaviors		Product mix
Financial projections		Roles and responsibilities
Funding requirements		Staffing and resourcing

These are just a fraction of the many things in your business plan that need to be reconsidered. Going through the process of updating your business plan will force you to consider all of the critical components necessary for navigating your way out of the impacts of COVID. It will also leave you with a tangible blueprint for how to create a future-focused sustainable reality for your business.

So, what are the core components of your business plan that should be revisited and updated?

Executive Summary

Your *Executive Summary* is really a macro overview of the entire plan. Try cover off as many of the following elements as possible:

- Background and context
- Business lifecycle maturity
- Capabilities and experience
- Goals and objectives
- Leadership and team
- Macro financial overview
- Mission statement
- Product offering

Despite appearing at the beginning, come back to your Executive Summary once you've completed all the other sections, as they will inform many of these elements.

Business Description

Your *Business Description* overviews what you do and the products or services that you offer. It should include:

- Competitive advantages
- Description of industry
- Industry sales
- Problems solved
- Target customers

Market Analysis

Your *Market Analysis* will help you better understand your industry, your place within it, and how to deal with future opportunities and threats. Make sure that it's as data-driven as possible, and include information on:

- Competitive analysis
- Customer profiles
- Industry description
- Industry outlook
- Industry standing
- Market size
- Target market

Organization and Management

This section overviews how your business is structured as well as who runs it and works within it. If you've recently downsized or brought on board any specialists with unique capabilities, it'll be important to update and note those changes here.

You should include:

- Bios and CVs
- Internal capabilities
- Leadership team
- Legal structure
- Organizational structure
- Roles and responsibilities

Products and Services

There's a good chance that COVID may have impacted your product mix and forced you to make changes to it. Provide granular detail around the goods or services you provide. Explain how these are different from those of your competitors. Include information on:

- Features and benefits
- Intellectual property
- Product mix
- Product lifecycles
- Research and development
- Suppliers and costs

Sales and Marketing

Your sales and marketing strategy will almost certainly have adapted to the new realities of COVID. Attracting new customers and keeping your existing ones will require new tactics and approaches. It is here that these should be outlined.

Include information on:

- Budgets and expected results
- Communication strategies
- Customer acquisition costs
- Distribution channels
- Growth strategies
- Marketing tactics
- Sales strategies
- Target markets

Operations Plan

Elaborate here on the specifics of how your business operates on a day-to-day level. You may have shifted focus in the things that you do or the ways that you work.

Other sections of your business plan focus on goals and aspirations, however this section should be focused on documenting the ways in which you work. Include information on:

- Costs
- Deadlines
- Facilities and equipment
- Inventory
- Locations
- Personnel
- Processes
- Suppliers

COVID revealed a number of supply chain vulnerabilities—especially for businesses reliant on international imports. When updating your business plan, make sure that you develop and document your inventory and supply chain risk mitigation strategies.

Funding Request

You may have previously sought funding to initially launch your business or fuel later growth projects. Now though, you may be looking for funds to support your cash flow or simply keep the wheels of your business spinning. If you are looking towards fundraising, include information on:

- Amount needed
- Capital utilization
- Creditor repayment plans
- Debt vs. equity
- Desired terms
- Financial statements
- Investor ROI
- Timelines and milestones

Financial Plan

The section of your original business plan that will have lost the most currency from since it was created until now is your *Financial Plan*.

To derive maximum benefit from having revised your business plan, try get as granular as possible with quarterly or monthly projections. Make sure to keep this section as data-driven as possible.

For Your Financial Plan, include:

- Balance sheets
- Capital expenditure budgets
- Cash flow statements
- Cash flow predictions
- Costs estimates
- Expected revenue
- Financial goals
- Income statements

Appendix

If you are the beneficiary of any COVID government stimulus programs or tax benefits, then there will be documents that outline terms, conditions and obligations. Many of these will have financial and/or legal obligations attached to them, which naturally have implications on current and future business operations.

Make sure to include these too as they obviously weren't relevant to your original business plan.

Improve Your Processes to Achieve Efficiency Gains

Cutting costs is a logical starting point for responding to the financial pressures caused by COVID. After all, if you can strip away expenses, you may be able to sustain previous operating margins even in the face of reduced sales.

However, what if instead of doing *less with less*, you were able to do *the same with less*? This goal becomes possible when you operate your business more efficiently.

Before diving into how to operate a more efficient business, it's important to take a step back and consider first the elements that comprise a business. Every business is fundamentally one big *system*. It is made up of *sub-systems* and *processes*...

Your *systems* are the 'big ticket items' that typically manifest throughout your individual business units. Examples include systems for sales, accounting and marketing.

Your *processes* are the step-by-step actions that are required to bring your systems to life. Examples include your manufacturing, delivery and invoicing processes.

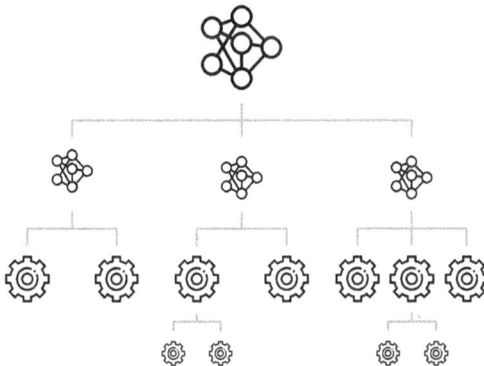

The number of processes a business possesses depends on its individual circumstances. For example, the size of the business, its industry and the nature of its offerings will all influence how many processes it has, and how complex each of those processes should be.

The totality of your systems and processes should all work towards attaining your business goals and objectives.

By breaking down your processes into discrete sub-processes, you're able to gain better visibility of the individual steps required to complete each of those processes. In many instances, this will illuminate process inefficiencies that are slowing you down and costing you money.

Businesses of all sizes should perpetually be on the lookout for processes that are...

Repetitive	Time-consuming	Complicated	Frustrating	Variable

Identifying inefficient business processes is especially important now. COVID will likely have impacted your business' operations, meaning that existing systems and processes may have been altered, or new systems and processes may have been introduced.

As examples...

Business Function	COVID Consequence	Process Impacted
Manufacturing	Reduced product mix	Production line
Operations	eCommerce sales channel added	Order fulfillment
Sales	Reduced headcount of sales team	Proposal development

So, how do you go about improving your processes to achieve efficiency gains?

Identify Opportunities for Process Improvements

Think about your business from multiple perspectives. Who are the relevant stakeholders and what processes do they currently (or need to) perform?

Identify tasks or activities that are repetitive, time consuming, complicated, frustrating or variable in nature. Following are some examples of processes and stakeholders that could be ripe for process improvements.

Example Process	Process Type	Example Stakeholder(s)
Strategic planning	Management Governance processes that ensure core business processes are operating effectively	Board of Directors
Customer onboarding	Operational Day-to-day processes that ensure the business' prime function(s) are being executed	Customer Service Representatives
Sales	Business Unit Business unit processes that ensure that a niche business task is performed	Salespeople
Order fulfilment	Cross-Functional Multi-functional processes that ensure that a key business task is performed	Accounting & Warehousing
Recruitment	Support Intra-business processes that aid the execution of all other processes	Human Resources

Document the Existing Steps

For existing processes, observe and record the sequential steps currently being undertaken to complete the task. Note seemingly mundane—but important—observations, like…

- Who's involved
- What they're doing
- Where they do it
- When they do it
- Why it's being done

Brainstorm Improvements With a Focus on Automation

In light of what you've observed, ask yourself whether any of the process steps seem unnecessarily laborious or burdensome on resources.

Does everyone need to be involved? Could anything be done quicker or better? Can you consolidate separate tasks or condense the times they take to perform? If there is no pre-existing process, think about the optimal steps that are required to complete it.

Technology presents you with unprecedented opportunities to automate repetitive tasks that previously demanded the time and individual attention of your team members. Nowadays you're able to replace many of these repetitive steps with automation technologies.

These tools help you reduce costs, increase productivity, decrease the frequency of mistakes, improve levels of customer satisfaction and become more agile.

Areas of your business you may want to consider using technology to automate include...

👍	Customer satisfaction	👥	Referrals
🛒	eCommerce	🪪	Registrations
🧾	Invoicing	🔔	Reminders
📣	Marketing	📇	Reporting
🔍	Recruitment	🏆	Sales

Gain Input From Key Stakeholders

Consult with key stakeholders like your team members. Ask for their input on why things are being done the way that they are. Elicit their opinions on whether things could also be done in a better or more efficient way. From *their* perspective, which processes (or steps) are repetitive, time-consuming, complicated, frustrating or variable?

Draft Updated Processes

Once satisfied with the extent of observations made and supplementary inputs acquired, draft updated (or new) processes that address the deficiencies and issues you've just identified.

Educate and Gain Buy-In

It's all well and good that you've identified inefficiencies and rectified them with updated processes, but the majority of these updated processes will inevitably be executed by members of your team—not you.

These are also the same people that have likely been doing things in a certain way, for a long period of time.

160

With that being the case, you'll need to do more than simply update the process on *paper*. You need to educate relevant team members on the updated processes too. This involves communicating not only *what* the new process looks like, but *why* it is being introduced. Explain what's in it for them and how it will improve their jobs.

With the right buy-in and understanding, you'll face less resistance on implementation, and increase the likelihood of the new processes' uptake and adoption.

Create a Home for Your Processes

There should be no ambiguity as to where anyone in the business goes for sourcing or reviewing the business' processes. Your documented processes should have a centralized home that is known to all. This is the go-to destination for anything and everything that concerns your documented processes—be it a physical or digital repository (or both).

Ensure Required Infrastructure and Resources are in Place

Regrettably, process improvement is not a 'sexy' undertaking. Despite noble outcomes, the *process of process improvement* itself is very much an exercise that's performed 'in the weeds'.

It involves thinking through all the micro details that need to come together to make the process work without a glitch. Anything less will result in a broken process.

It is incumbent upon you to ensure that all supporting tools and technology required by updates are in place by the time they'll be relied upon for activating any new process.

If you're making changes to your manufacturing processes, do you have the right equipment to produce the intended products? If you're adding an eCommerce distribution channel, have you set up a payment gateway on your website? And if you've scaled back the size of your sales team, who's now responsible for developing proposals?

Share Pre-Activation Communications

Once you're satisfied that you've gained buy-in and ensured that the necessary infrastructure and resources are in place, it's time to hit *play*. A critical success factor to ensuring a seamless new process roll-out is the pre-launch communications that go out to key team members.

Inform them of key dates and timelines, potential risks and mitigation strategies, as well as key role requirements and expectations. Use the communications as an opportunity to reinforce the reasons why this is all being done in the first place.

Amidst the volatility resulting from COVID, providing assurances and promoting certainty in the form of pre-activation communications will be noble and worthwhile outcomes.

Review and Adapt

Observe the updated process and its outcomes in operation. Thinking back to your initial goal of identifying process improvement opportunities, how much of an improvement have you gained with the *new* process from *old*? Are your assumptions and operational steps playing out as expected? And most importantly, have you actually achieved the goal of becoming more efficient?

Make sure to speak with key team members involved in running the new process. Find out whether there are teething problems, or perspectives on ways that the process can be further improved.

Don't feel wedded to the new process if it's proving to be sub-optimal—keep working at it till you get it *just right*. It may be a case of two steps forward, one step back, but eventually you'll get there.

Revise Your Organizational Structure for Smooth Operations

When we think about appropriate business responses to the impacts of COVID, we tend to think of initiatives like experimenting with new marketing tactics, scaling back your product mix, or pursuing new market opportunities; as examples.

Optimizing your organizational structure may not be on the radar of small businesses' efforts to respond appropriately to COVID.

However, fixing a sub-optimal organizational structure represents an efficiency play for your business. It's an opportunity to once again, 'do more' with 'the same'.

Aside from the efficiency gains, there are plenty of other reasons why you may wish to consider revising your organizational structure now…

- Clarify career progression pathways
- Define communication flows
- Delineate responsibilities and increase accountability
- Enable better decision-making
- Encourage idea sharing
- Improve planning processes
- Increase coordination and cooperation at all levels
- Minimize conflict
- Promote role and goal clarity
- Remove duplication of work

There's no shortage of organizational structure options available to pick from, nor is there a one-size-fits-all structure that's right for every small business. The 'right' structure is a function of many considerations. It should be determined after considering your options vis-à-vis *your* business and *its* needs.

Nonetheless, there are three popular structures for small businesses that have heightened relevance in responding to impacts of COVID...

Flat Structure

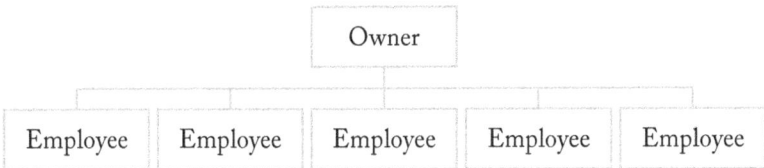

```
                        ┌──────────┐
                        │  Owner   │
                        └──────────┘
    ┌──────────┬──────────┬──────────┬──────────┬──────────┐
┌────────┐ ┌────────┐ ┌────────┐ ┌────────┐ ┌────────┐
│Employee│ │Employee│ │Employee│ │Employee│ │Employee│
└────────┘ └────────┘ └────────┘ └────────┘ └────────┘
```

Principle COVID Benefits:
- Eliminates middle-management as a cost-cutting measure
- Keeps a 'finger on the pulse' across the entire business
- Promotes quick decision-making and taking decisive actions

☑ **Key Requirement:** A capable and autonomous team

⚠ **Key Risk:** Lack of role and goal clarity

Functional Structure

Owner				
Marketing Manager	Sales Manager	HR Manager	IT Manager	Finance Manager
Marketing	Marketing	Marketing	Marketing	Marketing
Sales	Sales	Sales	Sales	Sales
Finance	Finance	Finance	Finance	Finance

Principle COVID Benefits:
- Promotes domain expertise as well as functional specialities
- Frees up owner's time to focus on more strategic matters
- Individual accountabilities and responsibilities are clearer

☑ **Key Requirement:** Well-defined decision-making processes

⚠ **Key Risk:** Siloed activity harming strategic alignment

Product Structure

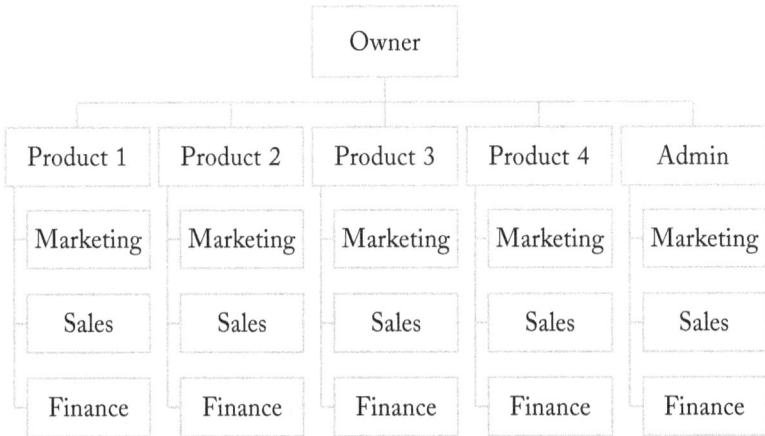

		Owner		

Product 1	Product 2	Product 3	Product 4	Admin
Marketing	Marketing	Marketing	Marketing	Marketing
Sales	Sales	Sales	Sales	Sales
Finance	Finance	Finance	Finance	Finance

Principle COVID Benefits:
- Business better able to manage priority product segments
- More targeted customer sales and servicing
- Adapt faster to market changes

☑ **Key Requirement:** Logical product segmentation

⚠ **Key Risk:** Duplication and resource inefficiency

Inevitably, there will be trade-offs with whichever organizational structure you decide to run with. The pros of one will be the cons of another. It is incumbent upon you to select the right organizational structure based on your circumstances of *today* and the goals you have for *tomorrow*.

The objective of re-building in the post-COVID period should factor high in your considerations and may make one particular structure more attractive than another. There's also a high likelihood that you'll stick with a structure not too dissimilar from what you currently have today.

Changes to your organizational structure is no mean feat and should only be undertaken in instances where there exist opportunities for material gains.

When revising your organizational structure for smooth operations, here are some considerations to keep front of mind...

Align to Your Strategy

Your post-COVID recovery period should be shaped by a revised strategy that leads you onto a path of renewed sustainability. Any revised organizational structure should prioritize this strategic objective. It should embolden your team as human resources to help them work in the most effective and efficient way. Think about your strategic goals with regards to your...

- Operational requirements
- Product mix
- Team skills and capabilities

Ensure that the resultant organizational structure will be appropriate for translating your strategic goals into action.

Consult Your Team

Speak to your team about your intentions to revamp the organizational structure and the motivation for doing so. Explain the options on the cards, relative pros and cons of each, and any considerations with regard to specific strategic objectives you hope to achieve.

Communicate the importance of their perspectives as key inputs, and the value they add in shaping these decisions as key stakeholders on the frontline of the business. Involving them as early as possible will increase buy-in when it comes to rolling out the changes they will have felt they've been a part of devising from the get-go.

Prioritize a Decentralized Chain of Command

During challenging times, you'll want to prioritize a chain of command that encourages shorter lines of communication. This will speed up your decision-making processes and provide autonomy and flexibility needed by team members to expeditiously put new plans into motion. It requires greater levels of team capability, but is equally an explicit sign of the trust you have in your team.

Obviously, flat organizational structures are more conducive to a decentralized chain of command. Regardless of the structure you elect, ensure that obstacles standing in the way of direct communications and efficient decision-making processes are minimized.

Determine How You Would Like Decisions to be Made

All businesses inevitably need to make decisions. These decisions get made by different team members sitting at different levels within the business. Even with a decentralized chain of command, good decision-making processes should be in place to recognize this reality. You'll want rigorous processes that produce reliable decisions. Has COVID resulted in needing to make any new decisions within your business?

Ensure that you consider decision-making processes when re-designing your organizational structure. If something requires senior oversight, review or approval; it should be captured in your organizational design.

Prioritize *Pragmatism* Over *Process*

Whatever organizational structure you land on, prioritize *pragmatism* over *procfess* wherever possible. This means eliminating convoluted lines of communication, burdensome admin formalities and unnecessary approval processes. Do not be beholden to old ways of doing things if they have proven to be ineffective or inefficient. In these challenging times you need to remain agile. This is best achieved by remaining unencumbered by needless obstacles that stand in the way of moving as quickly as possible.

Stocktake the Talent Within Your Team

Before you start divvying up roles and responsibilities and re-allocating these across your revised organizational structure, it's important to pause and take stock of the pockets of talent and areas of expertise that currently exist. This will be important in informing your decisions around how to appropriately restructure your business to capitalize on existing capability and mitigate areas of potential weakness.

Understand the Jobs to be Done

Since you have an established business, it's tempting to be thinking of your *people* first, and then work backward to allocate the tasks that needs to be done. But start by thinking about the *work* that needs to be done and then allocating the people best equipped to do it...

From   To

Turning things on its head in this way ensures that you're building a fit-for-purpose organizational structure that caters towards the workflow of things that actually need to get done.

This may require making compromises, hiring more staff, or up-skilling existing team members to address identified capability or capacity gaps. However, by doing things in this way, you avoid trying to retrofit workarounds when a better solution exists.

Ensure Workloads are Balanced

There'll likely be a re-shuffling of roles and responsibilities, and with that comes changes to workloads too. Make sure when revising your organizational structure, that sufficient attention is given to the respective workloads of individual team members.

Ensure that disproportionate workloads do not inadvertently fall on the shoulders of a select few, and that any disparity of balance is intentional.

During these trying and high-pressure times, individuals will want to feel that everyone is pulling their weight, and that contributions that go above-and-beyond the call of duty are recognized.

Document Responsibilities and Accountabilities

There's a cute story about four people: *Everybody*, *Somebody*, *Anybody* and *Nobody*...

> There was an important job to be done and *Everybody* was sure that *Somebody* would do it.
>
> *Anybody* could have done it, but *Nobody* did it.
>
> *Somebody* got angry about that, because it was *Everybody's* job.
>
> *Everybody* thought *Anybody* could do it, but *Nobody* realized that *Everybody* wouldn't do it.
>
> It ended up that *Everybody* blamed *Somebody* when *Nobody* did what *Anybody* could have.

Your organizational structure should document who is responsible and accountable for what. Even if some responsibilities and accountabilities are shared, it should be clear *what* expectations fall on *whos'* shoulders.

There may be new task requirements that didn't exist pre-COVID, resulting in natural ambiguity around who's actually responsible for getting these done. If there's an expectation that something's going to get done, make sure that those responsible for doing it are clear that it sits with them for ensuring that it happens.

Create Career Progression Pathways

Since you're asking more from your team, it's reasonable that they will be asking what's in it for them in stepping up to the plate. A natural answer is to 'climb the ladder' to aid and progress their career trajectory.

Having a well-defined organizational structure makes these pathways for career progression better-defined. It translates an abstract concept of *progression* into something more tangible that should serve as a motivating factor for increasing buy-in.

Make sure that defining career progression pathways factors into your thinking when making decisions that involve your team and organizational restructure. Be sure to communicate these exciting career progression opportunities that should motivate your team towards productive action and outputs.

Make Meetings Matter

Despite a consensus of frustration caused by meetings, they remain an essential ingredient of fruitful business operations. This fact does not negate the many ineffective and inefficient elements that are nonetheless involved in running meetings.

We *all* get irritated by inefficient meetings. We *all* get annoyed with meetings that involve individuals that don't need to be there. We *all* appreciate the opportunity cost of taking people away from better uses of their time.

With all the new pressures—on finances, resources and bandwidth—resulting from COVID, becoming efficient and making meetings matter is simply a non-negotiable.

As an example, consider a sample meeting that runs monthly, takes half a day, and requires four senior managers and two regular team members.

After checking with senior management, they confirm that the meeting need only run every second month. They acknowledge that half the meeting is spent socializing, and that they could easily get through all agenda items in two hours or less. They mention that on average, there are two non-managerial team members that are brought along to each meeting, who add minimal value and lack a connection to the topics of conversation.

Armed with this knowledge, you decide to make changes to this recurring meeting:

	Old	New
⌇ Frequency	Monthly $: 36,000 / ⏱: 288 hours	Every second month $: 18,000 / ⏱: 144 hours
◷ Duration	4 hours $: 36,000 / ⏱: 288 hours	2 hours $: 18,000 / ⏱: 144 hours
👥 People	4x Managers + 2x Others $: 35,000 / ⏱: 144 hours	4x Managers $: 28,000 / ⏱: 96 hours
Total	$: 107,000 / ⏱: 720 hours	$: 64,000 / ⏱: 384 hours
Savings:		$: 40% / ⏱: 47%

All figures are per year

As a result of these small changes, over the course of just one year, you've saved the business $43,000 in collective salary costs and 336 hours of additional productivity; and this was just from *one meeting*—imagine how much more there is to be won back across *all* your other meetings too!

COVID may have forced you to ask some important questions about meeting efficiency. There are big cost and time savings to be won through small changes you're able to make to your meetings' *frequencies, durations, personnel* and *purposes*.

So, how do you go about making meetings matter to achieve these wins?

Perform a Stocktake of Your Existing Meetings

Before you're able to make meetings matter, you first need to understand what meetings are currently taking place and how they are currently run. This involves doing a stocktake of the meetings that exist today, to tighten the reins on the efficiency and effectiveness of each of those meetings.

MEETING	Daily	Weekly	Monthly	Qtly	Yearly	Duration	Attendance
Manager One-on-One	✓					15 mins	Manager & Direct Report
Team Sales		✓				1 hour	Sales Team
Project Status		✓				1 hour	Project Team
Industry Update		✓				1 hour	Product Team
Coaching			✓			2 hours	Business Function Team
Solution Brainstorming			✓			3 hours	As Required
Resource Planning			✓			½ day	Snr. Mgmt. + 2x Team Members
Problem Solving			✓			½ day	As Required
Campaign Planning				✓		1 day	Campaign Team
Strategy					✓	2 days	All Staff

Clarify the Core Elements of Each Meeting

To make meetings run more efficiently and effectively, you have four major levers at your disposal. As you look through your list of meetings, ask yourself questions about each of those levers...

Lever	Description	Question
# Number	The number of meetings you run	Do we *really* need this meeting? ...or could it be run on an ad-hoc basis, only if required?
⋀ Frequency	The cadence that each meeting occurs	Do we need to run the meeting as often as we do?
◷ Duration	The amount of time each meeting takes	Does the meeting need to run as long as it does?
👥 People	The number of team members needed to attend each meeting	Who do we *actually* need to attend the meeting? ...with ability to bring in non-core individuals on an as-needs basis

Document the Meeting's *Purpose, Participants* and *Structure*

Now that you've clarified the different meeting levers you're able to pull to maximize efficiency and effectiveness, spell out the *purpose, participants* and *structure* for each of your recurring meetings...

Manager One-on-One Meeting

〰️ **Cadence:**   Daily

🕐 **Duration:**   20 minutes

Led By: Manager

💬 **Style:**   Informal & Collaborative

Participants: Manager & Direct Report

Discussion Topics:
- Current projects and their status
- Manager direction and feedback
- Issues and challenges

📖 **Pre-Meeting Requirements:**
- Manager to review performance-to-target data
- Manager to email any relevant pre-reading to direct report

Allocate a Meeting Owner

For true meeting effectiveness, it's important that every meeting has an 'owner'. This is the person with whom the buck stops for ensuring that the meeting is held for the purposes and with the structure that it is supposed to. Meeting owners take responsibility for ensuring that the meeting occurs with its intended frequency and for its proposed duration, and that all required participants attend.

Eliminate Distractions

These days it's not only hard to prohibit the use of technology in meetings, it may also be impractical. Whether laptops, tablets or smart phones; there's a pretty high likelihood that participants will be using one, two or all three of these.

Your goal is not to regress your meetings back to the stone age. It is to eliminate distractions and minimize the opportunity for these to rear their troublesome heads in your meetings.

If participants use any of these throughout the meeting, there needs to be an unspoken understanding that it's for the specific purpose of deriving maximum value from the meeting. Anything unrelated to that singular goal should not to be done whilst the meeting clock is ticking.

Enforce Pre-Meeting Preparation Requirements

How much time do you currently spend in meetings catching everyone up to speed on where you'd ideally have liked them to be at the time that they turn up?

This can be fixed by having the meeting owner take responsibility for ensuring that preparatory materials or pre-reading is distributed in sufficient time prior to the meeting taking place.

In addition to sending out preparatory materials, it is equally important there's an understanding that anything sent out prior to the meeting is expected to have been looked over too. Questions and comments should be brought to the meeting, with time set aside for answering and addressing these.

Ensure Meetings Run to an Agenda

You don't want to inhibit opportunities for an organic discussion that leads to positive outcomes. However, adhering to a meeting agenda will ensure that the meeting's purpose is kept on track as efficiently and effectively as possible.

The meeting owner should adhere to the meeting timelines. They should use the agenda to keep topics of conversation on focus, promote discussion around key ideas, and increase participation.

Keep Meetings Short

It may seem obvious, but meetings shouldn't be any longer than they need to actually be. Many meetings' durations are pre-chosen arbitrarily as a matter of convention, instead of the amount of time that discussions are expected to actually take.

These tend to be in *half-hourly* or *hourly* increments, which are big jumps, and not always necessary. Short and sharp meetings will focus the conversation, ensure that attention spans don't wane and prevent people's time from being wasted.

Document Action Items, Commitments and Next Steps

It's easy to feel that progress has been made simply by having a meeting. But it cannot be forgotten why the meeting occurred in the first place—to get stuff done!

The most important thing to come out a meeting is clarity around the action items that are agreed. These should be documented, with any time-bound commitments (*who*, *what*, *where*, *when* and *why*) also recorded. Commitments should be followed-up by the meeting owner after agreed timeframes following the meeting.

Avoid Scope Creep

It's common for meetings to get hijacked by additional topics of conversation. These may be well-intentioned and bring up some important points.

However, they are most commonly not aligned with the meeting's purpose, don't necessarily involve the majority of meeting participants and end up ultimately diluting the efficacy of the meeting.

When the discussion starts veering off purpose, call it out and park those discussions for another time or place. If need be, a separate meeting should be organized to take those discussions offline. These action items should be documented, and can be followed-up by the meeting owner after the meeting too.

Improve Internal Communications to Recognize New Realities

For many businesses, COVID disrupted their business-as-usual modus operandi. Typical ways of working were altered to accommodate slowdowns in business, forced store closures and government-mandated lockdowns. For many, working from home became the new norm. Regardless of the specific arrangement, communication amongst the team was put under strain.

Many businesses were quick to adapt, and did so quite well—especially in light of the limited time they had to prepare for the monumental shift. Despite the impressive adaptation, it still represented a new way of working. It brought to the surface the importance of good communication, and forced businesses to re-think how to maintain this goal moving forward.

Regardless of whether a full return to the office remains on the cards, businesses should use this opportunity as a time to optimize their internal communications, and there are many ways that they are able to do so...

Employ Active Listening
It starts with something simple. We often think of communicating as sharing things we wish to say with the people we wish to hear them.

However, *speaking* represents only half of the act. The other—arguably more challenging—half, is *listening*. Now more than ever it is critical that the perspectives of your team get shared, heard and heeded.

Active listening involves more than simply hearing what somebody else has to say. It is the process of offering your full attention to what that person is saying, to gain a more complete understanding of their message, intent and assumptions.

When done correctly, there are fewer misunderstandings, less frustration and faster realization of outcomes.

Determine if a Meeting is Actually Necessary

As we saw in the previous section, meetings are time-consuming, expensive and take precious time away from other important things—there's no shortage of other priorities going on right now that are able to fill your team's time!

Whilst sometimes you'll want to avoid email in preference for a short, sharp meeting, other times you'll want the exact opposite. Before setting a meeting, have team members answer the following questions...

Does the information actually need a voiceover, or is it self-explanatory?

Could information be given to select individuals to then be relayed onwards from one-to-many?

What 'pre-work' could be done to ensure meetings are short, sharp and to-the-point for those that must attend?

The answers to these questions should determine whether hosting a meeting is actually necessary, and if so, how information can be communicated in the most efficient and effective way.

Avoid Email if Appropriate

How many back-and-forward emails will it take to effectively communicate a particular topic of conversation?

Email is *not* the appropriate medium for anything that requires lengthy or detailed discussions. If your emails are likely to result in a drawn-out game of 'email ping-pong', reconsider whether an alternative method of communication should be used instead. How many reply emails could be avoided simply by picking up the phone and making a brief call instead?

Reserve email for short and purposeful exchanges of information. You're always able to follow-up succinct initial emails with calls and face-to-face meetings too.

Write Better Emails

Eliminating emails entirely is neither realistic, nor appropriate. Writing *better* emails is.

Replacing incomplete, ambiguous or confusing emails with short, sharp and complete messages will do wonders for improving your internal communications.

Compare the following...

Hi Michelle,

I thought you discussed lots of good points in that meeting and your suggestion was really good. I think we should explore its feasibility since the client expects us to come back with a proposal soon. I'm free to discuss this most times tomorrow.

Cheers,
Simon

VS.

Hi Michelle,

I thought your suggestion in the COVID recovery meeting to cut expenditure by 15% this quarter was really good. I think we should explore its feasibility—in particular key stakeholders, timeframes and budgets.

From our discussions with the client, we've committed to getting back to them by 5pm on Thursday at the latest.

Lets discuss the above feasibility issues tomorrow. Please send me a calendar invitation with whichever timeslot works best for you out of the following options: 10:00-11:00 am, 1:00-2:00 pm or 3:00-4:00 pm.

Feel free to also email me any questions you have beforehand and I'll do my best to turn up to our meeting with answers to them.

Cheers,
Simon

As you can see, trying to avoid ambiguity and pre-empt any questions for the recipient will act as a 'circuit-breaker' for the many inevitable follow-up emails that would have otherwise ensued. Through writing better emails, you're able to prevent issues, reduce frustrations and increase productivity.

Ask Better Questions

Writing better emails reflects only half the opportunity to step-up your communications game. In addition to writing better emails, you and your team are also able to *ask better questions*. Consider this as a second-tier 'safety net' for the times that initial communications are ineffective at sharing key information that needs to come across.

It's a framework we've been taught since grade school, but asking questions that answer the *who, what, where, when* and *why* will help work through ambiguities and get to the crux of an issue in the shortest amount of time…

- Who: People, stakeholders, teams
- What: Goals, KPIs, scope
- Where: Facilities, locations, markets
- When: Deadlines, milestones, schedules
- Why: Business case, motivations, ROI

Utilize Videoconferencing and Project Management Technologies

COVID lockdowns gave many their first real experience with videoconferencing software—who'd heard of *Zoom* prior to 2020?

Virtual meetings, workspaces and webinars are increasingly becoming the new norm; especially as the technology improves and more teams shift to flexible work arrangements.

In addition to videoconferencing software, consider improving collaboration with project management software tools too. It is vital that in your post-COVID recovery, you maintain focus on managing live projects and steering the business in the right direction.

Core features and benefits of project management software include:

- Automation of repetitive processes
- Balancing workloads fairly and evenly
- Evaluating progress with insights and analysis
- Gaining visibility of your sales and pipeline
- Kick-starting projects with more thorough planning
- Promoting better communication and collaboration
- Scheduling, forecasting and resourcing your projects
- Supporting remote working arrangements
- Tracking time, expenses and tasks
- Working from a central repository for files

Below are some leading project management software tools you may wish to consider. Some have free plans for small teams, or offer freemium versions, making them perfect for small businesses.

Airtable   asana   Basecamp   Jira Software   LiquidPlanner

monday   P Project   smartsheet   Trello   Wrike

Develop an Email Sorting System

The holy grail of email is achieving the coveted 'inbox zero'—the moment you've deleted every email in your inbox (and a proxy for having completed every outstanding task).

However, what you're truly shooting for is a system for prioritizing your emails that allows you to instantly categorize incoming emails into priority folders to be actioned according to their urgency and importance:

	Urgent	Not Urgent
Important	Urgent and important	Important, but not urgent
Not Important	Urgent, but not important	Not urgent, not important

Having your team prioritize their emails will cut through communication bottlenecks and expedite the rate that things get done. One popular system is filtering emails into separate folders that demand different responses. These responses include...

Replying to the email	Writing a separate email	Self-actioning a task	Delegating a task

Another popular system is sorting by the timelines that an email needs a reply (e.g. today, this week, this month, etc.).

Whichever system you run with, maintain discipline in adhering to your chosen system, and compliment this by unsubscribing from all non-essential email lists.

Promote Proactive Bottom-Up Communications

There's a tendency to think of internal communications as 'starting at the top' and trickling their way down to the bottom—for example, from the owner to on-the-ground staff, or project leads to team delegates.

However, internal communications should operate in both directions: top-to-bottom *and* bottom-to-top. Businesses should be encouraging the transmit of information *up-the-line* too...

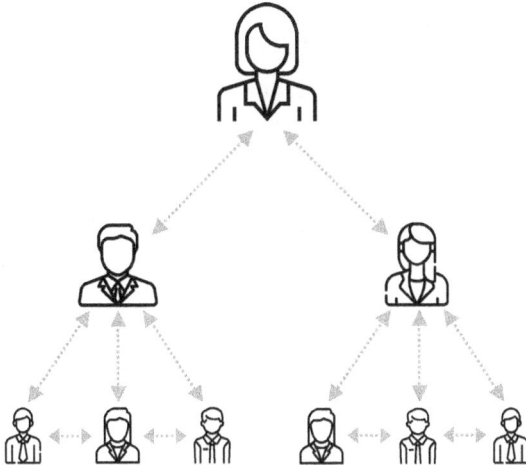

As those working at the coalface of your business, your team are the ones in constant contact with your customers and suppliers, and performing the nitty-gritties of day-to-day operations.

The post-COVID world has changed so quickly and materially, meaning that you cannot afford not to be hearing about what's happening on-the-ground by those in-the-know. Your team represent your eyes and ears for the 'word on the street', and are best positioned to be informants for the things you want to know about.

Team members should therefore be encouraged to think about internal communications as being a two-way street, and become accustomed to feeding information to whomever needs to know about it.

Batch-Process Questions and Discussions

There will be many times throughout the day that team members have questions for one another or ideas they would like to discuss. The ever-present temptation is to simply pop over to a colleague's desk the moment a question or thought enters their head.

It may not be intentional, but these seemingly innocuous interactions are actually disruptions to the focus of whomever is being engaged into conversation.

Again, you have a vested interest during these challenging times to optimize the efficient and productive outputs of everyone on your team.

Ideally—should the matter not be urgent—a list of discussion items and/or questions should be written down throughout the day, then 'batch-processed' at select times and in singular hits...

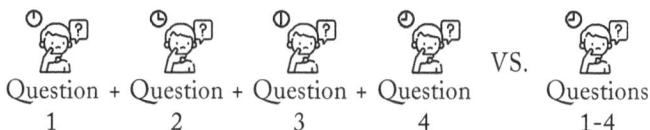

Question + Question + Question + Question   VS.   Questions
    1   2   3   4   1-4

This minimizes the number of disruptions that colleagues cause to one another. It also forces the list-maker to question whether they can get an answer through alternative means, thus becoming more self-reliant and developing problem-solving skills too.

Invest in Knowledge Repositories

To improve the development of self-reliance skills (and minimize disruptive communications), invest in *knowledge repositories*.

Very often, internal communications concern topics with consistent themes or that answer frequently asked questions. In the absence of knowledge repositories, the onus of answering these questions falls on the shoulders of team members. It is also not always clear who might have the answer to a question.

Knowledge repositories (like a business intranet) should be stacked with key resources and known as the go-to starting point for sourcing key business information. They can be as light or as comprehensive as you wish, but the more content they contain, the greater the likelihood they'll be used, and colleague disruptions minimized.

Case Study: Operations

Context

Tom runs a small tax and accounting firm.

When COVID hit, they initially experienced a wave of work in preparing submissions for tax subsidies. In many instances, they were unable to get through the workload volume in timeframes satisfactory to client expectations.

Tom came to realize that in addition to the increased size of the team, the firm's offering was substantially different today to when the business first started.

COVID also brought to the surface many issues arising from miscommunications and inefficiencies within the team.

Actions

Tom reviewed and updated his original business plan. This helped him appreciate the new competitive landscape, the firm's competitive advantages, and ways that these had changed the product mix and sales and marketing strategies from what they were once originally.

He reviewed many of the firm's internal processes, and spoke to his team members to better appreciate their perspectives on this too.

Coming off the back of this, he identified that tax subsidy submissions were not taking advantage of cheap automation technologies that would halve the time it takes to complete one of the most popular—yet time-consuming—services that the firm provides.

He also found that his client communication processes were tardy.

Tom revises his organizational structure to give it a more product-centric focus, whilst still prioritizing a decentralized chain of command to reflect its relatively small size.

Tom also introduces new protocols for running meetings, after identifying a large number of inefficiencies that were endemic in existing meetings as currently run.

Results

Tax subsidy submissions are now completed in one-third of the time they previously took to complete, freeing up an extra five hours per week for each team member that works on these.

Clients now receive their tax subsidies two weeks faster than before the new process was introduced, and client referrals for tax subsidy submissions have since doubled.

Less meetings, of shorter duration, now occur with fewer team members; resulting in boosts to productivity and team morale.

Team

Improve Results Through Better Performance Management

Drive Employee Engagement With Reward and Recognition

Become a Business Your Team Enjoys Working For

Maximize Productivity With Flexible Work Arrangements

Motivate Through Non-Financial Incentives and Benefits

Improve Results Through Better Performance Management

It's natural that you want to extract maximum value from your team members. Inevitably this requires checking in with them periodically to review their performance and ensure that it lines up with your goals, targets and expectations.

The impacts of COVID demand *additional* focus is placed on performance management. It is unrealistic to expect that your prosperous turnaround to stability will just happen by accident. The realization of your goals require a high-performing team, and *you* are responsible for unleashing that performance.

Your visions at the top must materialize into results at the bottom. This requires aligning your team with your performance expectations. Performance management allows you to do just that. During these post-COVID times, having a solid performance management framework will provide the following benefits...

- Attainment of business goals and results
- Clarification on what's important to the business
- Faster identification and resolution of problems
- Identification of capability and pockets of talent
- Improvements to team-building efforts
- Incentivization for goal alignment and achievement
- Increased employee engagement and productivity
- Increased personal accountability
- Optimization of employee value
- Strengthening of relationships

So, how do you go about improving results through better performance management?

Understand That the Goalposts Have Moved

Nobody in their wildest dreams could have foreseen the disruptions that would take place as a result of the COVID crisis. Budgets, targets and projections were decimated in the space of a few short weeks. Business owners have been left to adapt performance management frameworks on-the-fly.

It may not be appropriate to hold individuals accountable to pre-COVID goals, but this doesn't mean that *new* goals and targets should not replace these. Old *metrics*—if not the actual numbers and targets themselves—will likely remain the same, or very similar too.

Form a view around realistic—yet achievable—revised expectations. Now may not be the time for stretch targets, but current circumstances demand unwavering discipline in staying on a measured path of stability.

Share revised expectations in open and honest conversations, and elicit input on factors to be considered when devising new goals.

Increase Performance Management Intervention Frequency

There's a common misconception that performance management is a once-a-year event that takes form via the annual performance management review.

Whilst this review may be the pinnacle event on the performance management calendar, it should by no means be an isolated occurrence to the exclusion of other interventions.

In fact, more frequent check-ins of 'lesser' significance will count for much more than less frequent check-ins of 'greater' significance. Frequent performance management interventions permit easier in-flight adjustments *if* and *when* necessary. They provide a more accurate perspective of performance than could ever be achieved with an aggregated snapshot that tries to capture an entire year of performance.

The post-COVID recovery period is one of great uncertainty. There's a lot of questions without a lot of answers. It is critical that you increase the frequency of performance management interventions throughout these turbulent times.

More frequent check-ins will also provide you with a feedback mechanism for understanding gaps that exist between your recovery plans and their actual operationalization.

» Keep Performance Management 'Forward-Focused'

The traditional annual performance management review typically entails discussing key performance metrics for the year gone by, and comparing these against goals that were supposed to be hit. Beyond COVID's disruptions to goal attainment, this approach is not particularly instructive as to how relevant performance *improvements* are to be made.

Instead, consider *current performance*, and how this lines up with your future goals and targets. In this way, performance management becomes a forward-focused activity, rather than just a means of assessing how team members went in arriving at where you find yourself today.

Don't Forget to Find the *Good*

Current circumstances would be deemed difficult at the best of times, so it's important to recognize the operating reality your team are working within currently. It will be easy to find fault and spot all the things that *aren't* being done perfectly.

But so too will there be instances where persistence, passion and perseverance will also be on show. It is equally important to call *these* things out and provide explicit validation from the top that the hard work and toil is not going by unnoticed.

Individualize Performance Expectations

The unique capabilities of individual team members will be an important asset during these challenging times. Homogeneity of performance management approaches should be trumped by an individual, needs-based framework that recognizes the differing skills, strengths and weaknesses of individuals within your team.

Adopting a one-size-fits-all approach to your performance management framework will result in one-size-fits-all outcomes. This simply won't cut it at a time where you need agility and dexterity from your team.

Make sure that individual performance management plans set expectations that are commensurate with individual roles, levels of experience and current operating realities.

Remain conscious however, of maintaining relative consistency in your expectations across the team, to avoid accusations of double-standards or risks of team conflict.

Have a Conversation Around KPIs

Given the challenge of defining realistic targets in the aftermath of the COVID crisis, it becomes particularly important to have certainty on the key performance indicator *metrics* themselves.

These are the measures that will shortly have revised numbers wrapped around them. They will serve as anchors for having meaningful, evidence-based discussions on performance in the future.

It is preferable to have a smaller number of more important metrics than a larger number of less important metrics. Across the entire team, run through your KPIs and explain why you've deemed them worthy of tracking. This will help the team understand the things that matter most to the business—extra important at a time when strategic priorities may have been reset.

Explicitly Recognize Good Performance

Different people are incentivized by different motivators. Few however, don't appreciate having their hard work and efforts called out. You'll likely be making some big asks from the team. This may come in the form of long days, pay cuts or working outside of comfort zones. Don't underestimate the value of recognizing these sacrifices and investments.

Carve out dedicated time with both individuals and teams to recognize these things, and give public thanks for their contributions. You also don't need a formal calendar event to show gratitude to your team. Spontaneous, ad-hoc gestures of appreciation are likely to be those that mean the most.

When you see good work, call it out. When a team completes a project, let them know they've done a good job. When someone stays back to hit a deadline, remind them that their hard work has not gone unnoticed.

Doing so will foster a culture where everyone shoulders responsibility for business performance. Seeing co-workers get called out for their positive contributions will become an enviable outcome that many will aspire to attain for themselves.

Promote Job Security

Use performance management interventions as an opportunity to reinforce that your team members should feel safe in their roles.

With the COVID crisis, many people either lost their jobs or had job security diminished. To the extent that you're able to, providing reassurance in job security will avail fears that are naturally circulating in team members' heads during these challenging times.

It will also be a marker of empathy and leadership on your part, and signal to the team that you're *all in this together*. In doing so, it will provide greater entitlement of your requests for stepping up to the plate, and any sacrifices you're asking from the team in the short term.

Whilst performance management shines the spotlight on individual performance, your team's desire to outperform will be contingent on the longevity of tenure they see themselves as having with your business.

Introduce Performance Gamification

In this era of post-COVID recovery, the necessity for gaining a 'live' snapshot of performance has never been more important.

Gamifying performance enables you to do just that: you're able to elevate your most important KPIs and gain real-time feedback to track your success in hitting those targets.

Performance gamification is dynamic and forward-focused. Grounded in metrics, it eliminates accusations of subjectivity that typically accompany things like the once-a-year annual review.

Since all employees are able to engage in friendly competition with one another, it also raises the performance bar consistently across the entire business by incentivizing desired actions.

Gamifying performance can increase staff morale, job satisfaction and productivity—all benefits that couldn't come sooner at a time when everyone is likely feeling a little demoralized. It compliments reward and recognition programs you may have in place and provides opportunities for sharing good news stories too.

Make Performance Management About Teams Too

Performance management should maintain its principal focus on the individual. However new strategic directions and business-wide changes will also impact teams. In addition to one-on-one performance management interventions, make sure you dedicate some time to performance managing your teams too.

Now more than ever, collaborative approaches are required. Whilst you don't want to blunt personal accountability, *teams* need to understand their roles and responsibilities in contributing to the realization of new business goals.

This should alleviate feelings of 'heavy shoulders' as perceived by individuals, and encourage them to work as part of a high-performing team too.

Drive Employee Engagement With Reward and Recognition

Hopes for a prosperous and pleasant 2020 were quickly vanquished with the arrival of COVID in the early months of the year.

One of the virus' most challenging impacts was the emotional toll it took on individuals: job losses, social distancing, lockdowns, absences from friends and family—all compounded to make a bad situation even worse.

These are undeniably challenging times accompanied with a pervasive sense of general demoralization.

This context is the furthest place from where you'd want to be in driving your business towards goals of profitability and prosperity. Nonetheless, it is regrettably where we find ourselves today and it is outside anyone's control. What *is* within your control are the levers you're able to pull that influence employee engagement and morale. Rewarding and recognizing performance is one of those levers.

You can reward and recognize performance at the *business* level, like the work-life balance you provide to your team. You can reward and recognize performance at the *individual* level, like providing opportunities for career progression. In some instances, rewards will be financial, whilst in other instances rewards may be less tangible.

Ultimately, aspire to implement reward and recognition initiatives of all shapes and sizes. There's little to lose with a lot to gain...

Recognize Both Formally and Informally

Employee recognition should take place in both structured and unstructured contexts. Ad-hoc, informal 'in-the-moment' recognition heightens the authenticity behind the praise. It recognizes good work *when* and *where* it happens.

Conversely, formal recognition initiatives should be implemented too. These ensure that good work doesn't slip through the cracks, and that public forums are in place to shine a spotlight on these occurrences.

Embrace Rising Stars by Expediting their Career Trajectories

Reward good performance with opportunities to progress careers. This can take many forms. For example...

Fast-track access to learning and development opportunities that build new skills and provide additional qualifications

Encourage more experienced team members to play a mentoring role for new hires or less experienced co-workers

Ask team members to do a short presentation with the team on a recently-completed successful project or initiative

These small overtures are not only a de-facto recognition of team member capabilities, but could assist in alleviating large coaching loads that otherwise fall on your shoulders.

Reward *Values* and *Behaviors* Too

Whilst performance *results* may be easier to identify, it's also important to call out excellence when it comes to living your business' values or exemplifying model behaviors too.

When employees see values and behaviors elevated to more than just lip service, they will mobilize around the job of bringing them to life. This creates a virtuous cycle whereby the values you espouse increasingly become the values that are lived.

Introduce a Performance-Based Bonus Incentive Scheme

Your focus is to rebuild the business back to a state of sustainable profitability. Your team members are a key ingredient in enabling that objective. As principle drivers of the outcome, the team should also become beneficiaries of their toils and the fruits of their labors.

Dangling these incentives over the heads of ambitious team members will encourage buy-in and ownership in realizing goals.

Share Positive Customer Feedback

Every now and then, customers will proactively share feedback with your business. In some instances, a specific team member will be referenced. These positive testimonials and letters of thanks may come directly to you, a manager or any one of your other team members.

Make a habit of ensuring that this feedback is shared publicly with the team, so that the team member being praised can have a spotlight shined upon them. You're able to do this any number of ways—like forwarding a customer email amongst the team, discussing it at a team meeting, or spontaneously sharing it when it happens to come in.

Promote Peer Recognition

Business owners don't always have full visibility of activity taking place at the ground level. If recognizing performance were left exclusively up to you, there would be many times that it would slip through the cracks. In contrast, individual team members are well-placed to spot the good work of their colleagues.

Promote a culture that encourages team members to congratulate one another on a job well done. It will create an environment that takes excellence out of the shadows, boosts morale and fosters comradery. With increased public prominence, these overt recognitions are more likely to make their way up-the-line too. So, if you didn't know about them *before*, there's a better chance you'll find out about them *now*.

Use Gamification

As previously discussed, use gamification techniques to encourage your team to become more actively engaged in their work. Incorporate games into a framework that recognizes and rewards that engagement. This can take many forms, like displaying leader boards, setting challenges and recognizing performance through awarding points and badges.

207

Keep Records

In the same way that you'd record issues of under-performance, so too should you record instances of over-performance. Your ad-hoc moments of recognizing performance publicly should be simultaneously documented and recorded privately too.

Maintaining detailed records of instances that goals were surpassed or good behaviors exhibited will prove helpful down the track. Piecing together a composite picture of performance for forums like annual performance appraisals will rely on key inputs like these.

Recognize and Reward Across the Entire Team

There will naturally be team members that contribute more or less than others. This may be a result of their earnestness and work ethic, or may just be a consequence of their role and current realities.

Make a conscious effort to review the performance of the *entire* team, irrespective of who they are and what they do. Everyone plays a part in the realization of your post-COVID rebuild, and contributions to that end will take various forms. Call out good work performed by the entire team, including those lower down on the food-chain too.

Remember however, that differences in expectations are not a 'free pass' for under-performance at any level, and that any performance issues still need to get performance managed—regardless of with whom they sit.

In this way, recognizing and rewarding across the entire team will create the collective fabric required for moving onwards and upwards as a united and excited team.

Separate Praise From Criticism

Spontaneous instances of publicly recognizing performance should focus exclusively on calling out a job well done. Blending these with anything less will dilute the potency of the praise, and risks leaving an unintended bitter taste in the mouth of the recipient.

In future one-on-one forums like annual performance reviews, you'll have greater opportunity to discuss both the 'good' *and* the 'bad'. Team members will be more receptive to heeding feedback on both, being conscious of former efforts to isolate each accordingly.

Become a Business Your Team Enjoys Working For

Whilst it is tempting to pin your post-COVID recovery on simply becoming a business perceived as *enjoyable to work for*, it unfortunately requires more than simply just that—you'll still need consumer demand; you'll still need an excellent product mix; you'll still need satisfied customers; and you'll still need to make a decent buck.

Yet despite none of those things hinging *directly* on the 'enjoyment factor' of working for your business—in many ways—all of them do. Being a business that's enjoyable to work for lays a foundation for attaining the results you're looking to achieve…

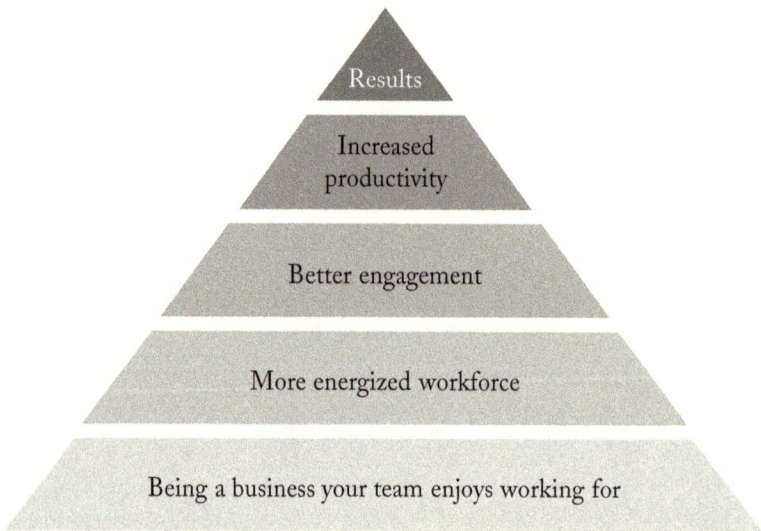

Results

Increased
productivity

Better engagement

More energized workforce

Being a business your team enjoys working for

Most measures required to become a business your team enjoys working for are neither expensive, time-consuming nor difficult to implement. With so much upside and so little downside, these initiatives represent the low-hanging fruit of your post-COVID recovery…

Promote Work-Life Balance

Balancing *work* and *life* is complicated at the best of times. Providing your team with flexible work arrangements will be a welcomed courtesy that demonstrates your efforts to be adaptive to their needs and boost job satisfaction.

Opportunities to eliminate the daily commute and working in casual clothing will be well-received gestures. Many teams had their first taste of such benefits during COVID lockdown periods, and now appreciate how desirable working this way can be.

Celebrate the Wins

In the daily grind of running a business, it's easy to forget to take time to celebrate the wins. These aren't just the big projects or major milestones—they are also the small day-to-day achievements that happen along the way.

Celebrating your wins has a greater role to play than ever before, as a mechanism for countering general demoralization stemming from COVID and its aftermaths. Whether it's ringing a symbolic bell or reporting up-the-line, these small acknowledgements of the wins will create an encouraging and contagious energy throughout your workplace.

Make Social Media… Social

It's easy to forget that your business' social media accounts are not just about rigid adherence to 'vanilla' corporate messaging. In fact, adopting this approach will deny your business many of the opportunities for communicating with your target audience in an authentic and relationship-building way.

Many customers are looking to connect with brands that are relatable and as true in real life as they claim to be on paper. You have the opportunity to share authentic insights into your business via posts, pictures, videos, or anything else that helps you connect with target customers.

Handing over the reins of your social media accounts—with clarity around expectations and standards—to your team, will inject some fun and color into their day-to-day existence. It will also provide your business with authentic content able to feed these accounts, which is often a challenge in its own right.

Create a Harmonizing Work Environment

Think about how much time your team spends in the office. Shouldn't this space ooze positive vibes and good feng shui? It may require a little investment, but don't underestimate the benefits of creating a space that is embraced by your team.

Creating this space will boost morale, increase productivity and harmonize the team with their surrounding environment. Whether or not its set-up requires external assistance, involve the team in building a space that they'll enjoy working in most.

Provide Small Perks and Treats

In addition to the physical environment of your workspace, consider also providing small perks and treats. The start-up world made this trend popular—introducing things like complimentary snack bars, catered lunches and dedicated chill-out rooms with comfy sofas and ping-pong tables.

These small gestures go a long way in breaking down old-fashioned stereotypes of what a workplace should feel like, and adds fresh excitement around the motivations for *wanting to go to work.*

Promote Structured Fun and Socialization

Every now and then, you and the team should have a social activity booked into the calendar. These can be for the entire business or done on a team-by-team basis.

Examples include lunch at a restaurant, an art class, or simply drinks and a boogie. To be perceived as benefits (not burdens) schedule these activities as much as possible within working hours. These small activities have the potential to make big impacts on morale—an important aspiration during these post-COVID times.

You're able to create social team 'taskforces' that are given the job of planning and running these activities, to create added buy-in and ownership. Consider also implementing a 'happy-hour' at the end of the work week, where time slows down and the team are able to enjoy a bit of at-work socialization too.

Create Exercise Opportunities and Provide Wellness Gestures

As the expression goes... *healthy body, healthy mind.* We're probably all well-aware of the benefits that are associated with being healthy. Many of these benefits transfer directly onto the workplace too.

Healthier employees are happier, less stressed and more productive. Employees should be discouraged from feeling like they need to make 'work' versus 'health' trade-offs. Some ways of reconciling this include…

Encouraging the team to get fresh air and walk around the block whenever they're in need of a brief 'time out'

Allowing your team to hit the gym or go for a run or stroll on their lunchbreak

Inviting yoga instructors or massage therapists to run group classes from within the office as an occasional treat

Encourage the Taking of Short Breaks

Your team should feel comfortable to take short necessary breaks—they're likely working harder than ever before! We all need the occasional respite, and no one enjoys feeling like their superiors are standing over their shoulders with a stopwatch every minute of every day.

As long as these breaks aren't abused, the reciprocal expectation is that work remains focused and productive. When exercised judiciously, these breaks should actually make for a more productive workforce.

Make the Most of the Holidays

The holidays represent festive times that are already primed to make people feel positive, energized and upbeat. Since they are often a big part of people's personal lives, and already front-loaded with goodwill and merriment, channel these positive vibes into the office energy too.

Doing a secret Kris Kringle present-swap for Christmas, decorating the office with 'spooky' props for Halloween, or eating some pumpkin pie for Thanksgiving are all examples of bringing some joy into the office under the banner of the holidays.

Celebrate Birthdays, Anniversaries and Key Milestones

It's nice to be acknowledged when key milestones take place. Things like birthdays and anniversaries (both personal and professional) mean something to the person that's celebrating them. When these occasions fall on a work day, it's easy for them to be forgotten or downplayed.

But it's just as easy to elevate them and make team members feel special—even if only for a brief moment. Celebrate these milestones and occasions with activities like...

- Being treated to the annual day off on your birthday
- Circulating a card to be signed by the entire team
- Decorating the team member's workspace
- Enjoying a glass of champagne
- Taking five minutes to cut a cake with the team

These small gestures go a long way in showing consideration to the personal lives of your team, and demonstrate your desire to make the workplace as personable and pleasurable as possible.

Maximize Productivity With Flexible Work Arrangements

COVID was a crisis of unfathomable consequence. It caused disruptions to every facet of our lives, and left ripple effects in the most unexpected of places. Leading examples include *where* and *how* we work. Early efforts to slow down the spread of the virus meant that offices were shut down and employees told to work from home. Literally overnight, with little-to-no planning, small to large workforces were told to pack up, go home, and continue to work.

At first, there was a certain novelty to it. Very quickly though, this novelty turned into the new norm. The cubicle desk was replaced with the kitchen table. Meetings in the conference room were replaced with videoconference calls over the internet. And long daily commutes were replaced with winning back hours from each day.

There were definite challenges, trade-offs and new learnings required; but by-and-large, we adapted, survived, and in many instances, thrived. It demonstrated that there was an alternate way to how we'd worked in the past.

The question before us now, is what learnings are we able to take from this experience into the future?

In the lead-up to the COVID crisis, many businesses had begun dabbling in *flexible work arrangements*. What are these?

Hours of Work	Patterns of Work	Locations of Work
Example: *Start and finish times*	Example: *Job sharing*	Example: *Working from home*

Introducing flexible work arrangements stands to benefit both you and your employees. Employees are grateful for the additional flexibility, and often find these new arrangements both novel and refreshing. For the business, they appeal to a demoralized workforce, create new efficiencies and can raise the bar on productivity.

So, how do you set up flexible work arrangements that maximize productivity for your business and your team?

Have Your Team Create a Quiet Space

Given that communication is key and team members will likely be fielding their fair share of voice and video calls from outside the office, it's important that a dedicated 'quiet space' be set up at their homes. The last thing anyone wants in the background of a call is a crying baby or neighbor mowing the lawn!

Set up Appropriate Home Workstations

It's fine that your team members work from their kitchen tables when it's the once-a-year sick day. But when working from home is part of the regular routine, a workspace as similar to what's in the office should be set up. This includes a clean desk, computer, ergonomic chair, and all the technology and stationery that's required to do their jobs.

Increase the Frequency of Check-Ins

For each of the benefits of providing flexible work arrangements, there is an equal and opposite challenge. Flexible hours, patterns and locations of work may provide additional benefits; but come with the challenges of managing a decentralized and remote workforce.

Whilst not a problem per se, this reality implores greater diligence in being an effective manager that checks-in with team members on a more frequent basis. Ensure that they're setup to succeed and are unimpeded by efficiency obstacles that are a consequence of being out of the office. Make sure that the benefits of flexible work arrangements aren't offset by diminished productivity that come as a consequence.

Separate Work Time From Personal Time

Just as personal life shouldn't invade working life, so too must the personal lives of your team remain protected from the demands of their work commitments.

An ordinary work day is clearly demarcated by the physical act of *entering* and *exiting* the office. This symbolic activity doesn't take place when the team works from home. If working from home is to become part of a normal routine, then unequivocal demarcations must exist between the 'professional' and the 'personal'.

Ensure a Good Internet Connection and Address IT Security

It's near impossible these days to work without an internet connection. The last thing anyone wants is to be dragging their feet with patchy internet that keeps dropping out.

If working from home is to become a frequent occurrence, ensure that your team use a reliable ISP (Internet Service Provider) in their homes. You should also consider investing in a Wi-Fi booster if signal strength is likely to prove to be a problem.

Videoconference calls can place big strains on bandwidth limits. Therefore, ensure that a sizable data plan sits alongside a reliable ISP and good signal strength too.

Access to any relevant work VPNs (Virtual Private Networks) should be set up with the business' IT support, who should also be comfortable working through any IT issues from people's homes too.

It's important that IT security considerations are baked into any work from home arrangements as there are additional security risks that result from team members working remotely from different locations. You should discuss potential IT risks with your IT support and develop appropriate risk mitigation plans that address these.

Set Daily Agendas

Working from the office may be replete with inefficiencies, but it still wraps a layer of structure around the day. Working from home often lacks this structure.

Have team members start their day by setting out a high-level agenda for what they plan to accomplish by close of business. In addition to promoting self-accountability for making the best use of their time, these agendas are also principle assets for the one-on-one check-ins you'll be carrying out with greater frequency.

Encourage the Team to Get Out of the House

When working from home, it is entirely possible that an entire day's movements comprise walking between the bedroom, bathroom and kitchen.

For the sake of your team's health and sanity, encourage them to occasionally get out of the house, reset the clock and get the blood pumping—even if that involves just a walk around the block or grabbing a quick coffee.

Be Cautious When it Comes to Multitasking

When it comes to multitasking, just because you *can*, doesn't mean you *should*. Especially when working from home, there'll be countless opportunities to do multiple things at once—whether work-based or personal.

The benefits of working from home should be the *increased* efficiencies gained. Don't negate these by allowing the team to fall into the trap of thinking they're able to bite off more than they can chew.

Maintain a Physical Presence

Of all the downsides of flexible work arrangements, one of the greatest is the decreased frequency of organic face-to-face interactions that occur.

Office interactions are made possible by having the same people simply occupying the same physical space. These 'watercooler' moments are conducive to creating a workplace momentum that fosters collaboration and business outcomes.

In their absence, purposeful measures and proactive efforts are required to compensate for not always being in each other's physical presence. Maintaining the sense of a 'team' will be much harder without physical interactivity being an integral component of your operating dynamic.

A simple way of addressing this conundrum is to ensure that your team maintain a physical, 'real-world' connection every now and then. If flexible work arrangements are to become a common occurrence, then it is important that team members retain some degree of actual facetime with one another.

For all the benefits of working remotely, there's no substitute for human interactivity. Weekly or monthly face-to-face catch-ups—whether professional or social—will be vital for the sustainability of effective flexible work arrangements.

Exchange Extended Work Hours for Time Off In Lieu

Flexible work arrangements are not limited simply to allowing your team to work from home. Because of COVID, many businesses have needed to ask their team to go above-and-beyond the call of duty, often resulting in working extended hours.

In the past, it was easy to dismiss extended work hours as coming out in the wash with all of the times that extended breaks or shorter days may have been worked.

However, if team members have been, or are going to be, working extend hours; consider recording this as *Time Off In Lieu*, whereby team members accrue paid time off in recognition of their added labors.

Motivate Through Non-Financial Incentives and Benefits

Over the coming months of your post-COVID rebound, you'll be asking a lot from your team. These requests will come at a time that follows personal stresses they will have felt as a result of COVID and its impacts.

Purse strings will have tightened, pay cuts may be in effect, job security may be at its lowest, and bonuses are far less likely to be on the cards. With all those things combined, it's natural there'll be a dip in team member morale.

The levers at your disposal for addressing this may feel limited. In better times, increasing salaries or providing financial remuneration may have been be a natural starting point for incentivizing team members. However, the current climate may make such options prohibitive on your end. It is also not the only solution.

Consider other *non-financial* incentives and benefits you're able to offer. Many are initiatives that your business would benefit from in good times *and* bad—now might simply be the trigger for putting them into effect.

During these challenging times, the relevance and timeliness of non-financial incentives could not be more appropriate. Activating them now will be a testament to your leadership and the motivating efforts you're driving to level-out the volatile environment you find yourself in.

Following are some non-financial incentives and benefits you're able to offer your team for encouragement and motivation...

Utilize Public Recognition Events

Take the time to publicly recognize great work being done by your team. Public recognition events will validate that their efforts and contributions are valued and appreciated.

There's a wide range of options for how this can be achieved, including things like...

🏆 Annual award ceremonies

🍽 Monthly lunches

👥 Weekly catch-ups

Institute Rostered Days Off

There's a good chance that your team are working hours above-and-beyond their contractual obligations. They're probably also tired and in need of a small boost to morale. If the pipeline's a little light, or workflow permits it, consider implementing *rostered days off.*

These are designated days in a roster period that an employee doesn't have to work. You're able to stagger these within the team to ensure you maintain sufficient coverage in the office.

Rostered days off will be well-received, and are likely to result in team members becoming more thankful and productive employees on all of the other days that they *are* working.

Grant Extra Annual Leave

For a number of different reasons, it may not be practical in your business to provide rostered days off. Rostered days off might also only be feasible for some roles, but not others.

For all the reasons you may wish to provide team members with rostered days off, it may make more sense to provide them with extra annual leave instead.

Team members may actually have a preference for this, as a post-COVID vacation may feel like the exact type of rest and relaxation they're looking for after everything that's gone on this year.

Provide Gifts as a Show of Thanks

Consider giving small symbolic gifts to team members. These tokens of appreciation recognize contributions that go above-and-beyond the call of duty.

Using your familiarity with the team, you're able to determine which gifts will be most appreciated by different individuals. A few popular options include...

- Bottle of scotch
- Bouquet of flowers
- Fine dining experience
- Gift cards
- Spa treatment
- Tickets to a show

Having a larger number of small value options will enable you to recognize and reward more team members on a more frequent basis.

Facilitate Time With Management

Management often default to providing team members with the minimum one-on-one time required to simply keep the wheels moving. However, team members often relish the opportunity to maximize their access to management.

There needn't be a formal agenda, nor any specific outcome in mind—a simple offer for an informal catch-up will likely represent an unexpected—yet much appreciated—gesture.

Team members should feel free to chat about whatever is on their mind—personal *or* professional. Make sure individuals understand they're able to share anything, and that everything discussed is naturally confidential.

Team members' sense of importance will be elevated, whilst you also gain opportunities for candid feedback that help keep a finger on the pulse of your business too. This mutually-beneficial result represents a covetable outcome in these challenging post-COVID times.

Enable Leadership Opportunities

There's never been a better time to provide leadership opportunities to your team—there's lots to get done and limited hands to do it. Much activity likely involves new initiatives that have come into play as a result of COVID.

All of these require someone to take ownership and drive things forward. Elevating your team members to positions of leadership is an explicit demonstration of the trust you place in them and their capabilities.

A natural corollary of this trust is inferred *job security*. Team members internalize the principle role they play in fulfilling the business' mission, and you gain a litmus test for validating leadership plans and initiatives.

Create Time for Passion Projects

If time permits, provide your employees with the opportunity to initiate business projects and initiatives that they come up with. These may be ideas that have lingered in their minds for some time, but been de-prioritized because of bandwidth constraints.

Setting aside a few hours of the work week to pursue these initiatives will symbolize the trust you place in your team's judgement, and elevates the responsibilities you're prepared to place on their shoulders.

The work is likely to be highly enjoyable and bear fruitful and innovative outcomes that may just end up becoming part of your profitable business-as-usual activity too.

Support Professional Development Opportunities

Your team should be hungry for professional development opportunities and now may be the perfect time to be providing these to them. In addition to up-skilling your team with new capabilities that benefit your business, these formal learning interventions represent opportunities for buttressing an individual's professional credentials too.

Opportunities for learning and development therefore not only benefit *your* business, but also make your team members feel like more valuable contributors to the business.

Offer Flexible Work Arrangements

As touched upon in the previous section, working from home became a common practice with the peak of the COVID crisis. It opened the eyes of many businesses to the fact that alternative ways of working needn't equate to a reduction in productivity or quality of outputs.

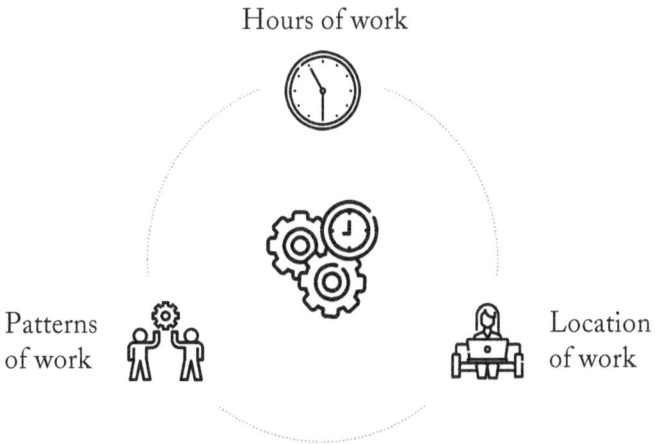

Hours of work

Patterns of work

Location of work

In many cases, these were actually enhanced: reduced commute times, less distractions and the novel enjoyment of working from home are all benefits that are frequently appreciated.

It may not be practical to have a permanently de-centralized team, but offering flexible work arrangements—like the hours, patterns and locations of work—should be welcomed by those to whom it is offered.

Allow Flexible Work Hours

As just discussed, the *hours of work* is one element of potential flexible work arrangements.

COVID impacted both personal and professional spheres of life. Individuals and businesses needed to respond with a flexible and dynamic approach that recognized these imperfect conditions: parenting responsibilities remained; groceries needed to be bought; pets still needed to be walked.

All of these day-to-day mundane tasks that were previously relegated to the 'outside-of-work' sphere of life, now needed to co-exist with work responsibilities and commitments.

For some jobs, flexibility around work hours may not be possible. For example, waitstaff or retail salespeople will need to work fixed shift hours. However, for many other jobs—in particular office-based professions—there may be flexibility around the hours in which the work actually needs to be done.

So long as there's an understanding that the job will get done and the required hours worked, allow flexibility around the specific times that these hours need to be clocked.

Case Study: Team

Context

Danielle runs a local nail salon.

When COVID hit, the salon was forced to shut-down for three months. Upon reopening, they have been busier than ever, with customers excited to utilize beauty services once again.

Danielle's team have been working around the clock to satisfy customer demand. They are working longer shifts than they would otherwise like, and are starting to feel burnt out.

They also fear that it's just a matter of time until the next government-mandated forced shut-down, and are therefore fearful of losing their jobs.

Actions

Danielle set time aside to meet individually with each one of her team members.

She acknowledges how demanding the current situation is, and thanks each of them for all of the extra effort they've tirelessly put in.

She talks about her post-COVID expectations, and makes sure that everyone is on-board. She also stresses the importance of work-life balance and her willingness to assist in any way that she's able to.

As a show of thanks for the extra effort everyone has been putting in, Danielle gives the team an additional three days of annual leave.

She also organizes to send team members on a two-day beautician's course to advance their formal qualifications—something Danielle knows team members have requested for quite some time now.

Danielle receives multiple compliments for her beauticians from customers, and shares this feedback with the entire team during their weekly team lunch outings on Fridays, which she sponsors.

She's also created a 'Social Media Taskforce' who are responsible for profiling the business and helping to rebuild the salon's brand online.

Results

As time goes now, the flow of customers returns to a more manageable pace, and regular hours of operation return too.

Despite recent events, staff morale is at an all-time high, and team members are voluntarily offering to swap shifts to assist one another meet conflicting personal commitments.

In the space of just a few months, the salon's Facebook page have doubled their number of followers. Many new customers announce this as being how they first found out about the business.

Accounting and Finance

Prepare for the Future With Budgeting and Forecasting Tools

Stay on Track With Key Performance Indicators

Build Sustainability by Managing Your Cash Flow

Understand Debt Finance Options to Carry You Through

Government Assistance Measures to Help You Out

Prepare for the Future With Budgeting and Forecasting Tools

Historically speaking, there was an air of certainty and predictability around the ways that your business operated. You knew...

What you sold ...	Who you sold it to...	How much you sold it for...	How often these things got sold

There may have been small variances year-to-year, or changes with a competitor entering or exiting the market; but barring factors like those, the state of play was more or less predictable in nature.

Why this matters is that *predictability* may have enabled *complacency*. Rightly or wrongly, you were probably familiar enough with your business' finances to make some broad-brush assumptions of future performance based on past performance.

The expectation of past performance being an indicator of future performance may have resulted in 'shortcuts' being taken when it came to budgeting and forecasting. Even when budgets and forecasts *were* diligently prepared, there's a good chance they revealed insights not too dissimilar to what was intuitively felt in your gut.

That reality has now changed for many small businesses. Accurate financial budgets and forecasts are no longer just 'nice-to-haves'. In many ways, old financial assumptions no longer reflect new current realities.

Because of COVID, the *economy* has changed; *markets* have changed; *customers* have changed; and your *business* will have changed. If ever there was a time to doubt your assumptions, unfortunately it is now.

What then, is the solution?

A reversion back to data-driven, evidence-based *budgets* and *forecasts*.

Just as you'd check the weather forecast to decide if you'll need an umbrella tomorrow, so too should you check your budgets and forecasts to understand what lies waiting around the corner for you and your business.

You may already be familiar with the many fruits borne from good financial clarity. In these post-COVID times, these become *extra* important. Developing budgets and forecasts will help you...

- Allocate resources
- Determine financing needs
- Grow your business
- Identify overspending
- Improve profits
- Increase ROI
- Make strategic decisions
- Manage your pipeline
- Predict cash flows
- Reduce costs
- Spot risks
- Track performance

So, how do you prepare for the future with budgeting and forecasting tools?

Utilize Both *Budgets* and *Forecasts*

Despite being complementary, *budgets* and *forecasts* are not the exact same thing. They serve similar, but different purposes:

	Budgets	Forecasts
Illuminate your...	Aspirations	Estimations
Help you...	Decide where to go	Understand where you are going
Are updated...	Annually	Weekly or monthly

Budgets are *aspirational*, and activated by plans that are wrapped around them. Forecasts are *estimates*, and are useful for modelling different scenarios that reflect contemporary circumstances.

Both therefore serve critical purposes in helping you stay grounded and focused in responding to new COVID realities.

Be Discerning When Extrapolating From Past Assumptions

Previously, you were able to rely on your prior financial performance as a key input in building budgets and forecasts. The impacts of COVID may render data on past performance of limited relevance for use in budgeting and forecasting processes—current operating realities may simply have changed too considerably.

Nonetheless, don't throw the baby out with the bathwater. Segment the areas of your business that were financially impacted by COVID (e.g. cash flows, sales volumes, etc.) from other areas of your business that have been less impacted (e.g. fixed costs)...

Rent	Cash Flow	Salaries	Sales	Taxes

Using past income statements, cash flow statements and balance sheets will prove a useful starting point for identifying the areas of your business that were impacted, from those that were not.

Undertake Complementary Independent Research

COVID created many new uncertainties, any of which could throw a major spanner in the works to budgets and forecasts if you continued to operate without updating assumptions that reflect new realities.

Where past results are unable to inform future expectations, you'll inevitably need alternative inputs to compensate for this limitation. This is best achieved with fresh and rigorous independent research.

Independent research is the antidote for arriving at logical new assumptions needed to inform your forecasts and budgets. Things you may wish to reinvestigate include:

- Average customer sales
- Customer acquisition costs
- Market size
- Purchasing trends and behaviors
- Your market share

Involve Your Team

Your budgets and forecasts will be strategic assets that are relied upon heavily by you and your team. It is therefore incumbent upon *you* to ensure that you arrive at a good outcome.

However, *driving the process* is different to *going it alone*. In fact, attempting to determine many of these new assumptions without the input of key team members will create new risks around their reliability and accuracy.

Your team are the ones on the coalface of the business day-in and day-out. *You* may know your business better than anyone else, but there's no way you know it better than the combined familiarity of your entire team.

In addition to using the team to build new assumptions, use them to sanity-check any new assumptions once built too.

Record Your Assumptions

Having undertaken your own independent research and involving your team, you should arrive at new assumptions that will inform the inputs necessary for updated budgets and forecasts. Drop these assumptions into your suite of financial statements, that include your...

Income Statement	Balance Sheet	Cash Flow Statement

It is very important that you record your assumptions. Your forecasts should be dynamic and living documents that are easy to update as new information comes in. Your budgets should reflect realistic expectations that are grounded in data of what's probable or likely. For both of these reasons, you'll want to know how you arrived at the numbers that you did.

Create a Dynamic Tool

As was just noted, budgets and forecasts are laden with assumptions. The purpose of these financial tools is to inform strategic plans and make better operational decisions. You'll appreciate this as you navigate your way out of the financial uncertainties created by COVID. It is therefore critical that as better information comes in, that it finds its way into your budgets and forecasts.

However, the fog of COVID will have made accurate budgeting and forecasting even harder. You'll want the ability to update your assumptions quickly and simply in a way that any updates cascade seamlessly throughout all relevant financial statements.

Since new information may vary and present itself sporadically, your budgeting and forecasting tools need to be adaptive and dynamic. Being beholden to inaccurate budgets and forecasts may steer you down wrong paths and lead you into making ill-advised decisions.

Track Your Budgets to Actuals

You'll invest a lot of time in determining new assumptions to build your budgets. Your budgets indicate the flag on the hill for where you aim to take the business. You should invest the same energy in analyzing how you *thought you would go*, with analyzing how you *actually went*.

This is done by comparing your *budgeted* performance against your *actual* performance. In doing so, you'll see what you got right, what you got wrong, and just how big the gap between 'right' and 'wrong' actually was. These gaps may illuminate business blind spots, like seasonal trends or supply chain vulnerabilities. And if nothing else, this knowledge will assist reaching more accurate assumptions for future budgeting processes too.

Identify Drivers of Revenue

It's a far easier task to estimate future *expenses* than it is to predict future *sales*. Your best bet in addressing this challenge is to make an exhaustive list of every *revenue driver* you're able to think of.

Think through your entire product mix, the marketing activities you undertake and distribution channels you have in place. Overlay this with your research on market size, buyer behavior and any sales cycles or seasonality factors too.

Since so much of budgeting and forecasting relies on the accurate assumptions you land upon, identifying all potential drivers of revenue will be key to achieving that objective.

Model for Best, Base and Worst-Case Scenarios

Given the depth of uncertainty in the post-COVID world we now live in, the room for budgeting and forecasting error is large. One way to mitigate this, is to model out multiple scenarios that reflect the *range* of realities your business may experience...

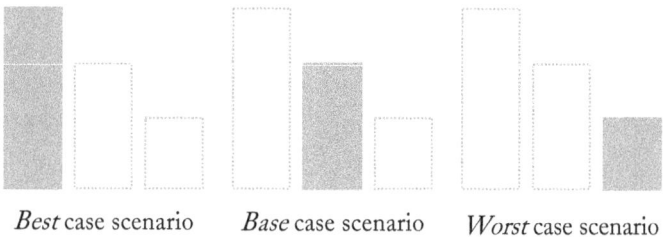

Best case scenario   *Base* case scenario   *Worst* case scenario

Modelling various scenarios should not represent a shortcut for being any less scrupulous when determining your assumptions. It simply acknowledges the many assumptions on which your budgets and forecasts are built, and the impossibility of predicting every future scenario *exactly* as it will play out.

Off the back of this, you can create different plans for different scenarios—making sure that you're far less likely to be caught off guard for a future scenario you hadn't previously considered.

Make Better Business Decisions

To derive maximum benefit from having developed your budgets and forecasts, you'll want to interlink the two as much as possible—sharing common assumptions, figures and interdependencies.

Any plan, project or long-term initiative of the business should reference your budgets and forecasts as the ultimate 'source of truth' when sourcing assumptions required for relevant planning processes.

If discrepancies emerge between what the business is seeing in its day-to-day operations and the figures found in your budgets and forecasts, then consider whether your underlying assumptions need to be corrected. In this way, you're perpetually validating your assumptions and improving their accuracy and reliability.

Stay on Track With Key Performance Indicators

At the best of times, your business is the sum of countless moving pieces that intersect against a backdrop of ever-changing market conditions and consumer behaviors. As if managing things weren't hard enough already, COVID overlayed this operating environment with new disruptive elements that delegitimized many historic assumptions too.

There's little doubt you've already been running your business with some degree of attention to Key Performance Indicators (KPIs). At minimum, you monitor your sales and costs, and make sure the business brings in enough to cover its expenses.

However, now more than ever it's important to be disciplined in tracking your KPIs. You can no longer afford to simply have 'fuzzy' understandings of your business' performance. With old assumptions now being less reliable, the consequences of mistakes are far more impactful.

Tracking financial KPIs in post-COVID times becomes essential as they help you...

- Benchmark your successes and failures
- Build a roadmap for realizing business goals
- Gain business insights from different perspectives
- Identify where and when any problems may exist
- Understand how your business is actually performing

Remember—you can't manage what you don't measure.

The following are ten financial KPIs that are helpful for gaining a composite view of your business' performance to help you navigate your way towards better times...

Operating Cash Flow

Your *Operating Cash Flow* (OCF) is the amount of cash generated by the operating activities of your business. It lets you know whether you are making enough money from your operations to pay the bills, and indicates the financial stability of your business' operations.

$$\text{Operating Cash Flow} = \text{Net Income} + \text{Non Cash Expenses} - \text{Increase in Working Capital}$$

If OCF is small, your business may require external financing.

Gross Profit Margin

Your *Gross Profit Margin* (GPM) is the amount of money left over from sales after subtracting the cost of goods sold.

For example, if you had a GPM of 35%, then 35% of your total revenue became gross profit. It indicates sales and production performance, and your business' general financial health. A higher GPM suggests efficient processes, whilst a lower GPM would suggest inefficient processes.

$$\text{Gross Profit Margin} = \frac{\text{Revenue} - \text{Cost of Goods Sold}}{\text{Revenue}} \times 100$$

Net Profit Margin

Your *Net Profit Margin* (NPM) is the amount of profit generated as a percentage of your revenue.

It tells you whether your sales are generating enough profit, and whether you are effective at containing your operating and overhead costs.

NPM is therefore useful for knowing how much of each dollar of revenue has translated into net profit.

Since so much of budgeting and forecasting relies on the accurate assumptions you land upon, identifying all potential drivers of revenue will be key to achieving that objective.

$$\text{Net Profit Margin} = \frac{\text{Revenue} - \text{Cost of Goods Sold} - \text{Operating \& Overhead Expenses}}{\text{Revenue}} \times 100$$

If your operating expenses are increasing at a rate faster than your revenue growth, then your NPM will shrink.

Revenue Growth Rate

Your *Revenue Growth Rate* is the percentage increase or decrease in revenue over time. It indicates your business' propensity for sustainably making money, by showing how well it is able to grow its sales revenue.

$$\text{Revenue Growth Rate} = \frac{\text{Revenue in this period}}{\text{Revenue in previous period}} \times 100$$

Revenue Growth can be particularly helpful if it is calculated for different products or product lines, as it can highlight which products are most responsible for revenue growth or decline.

Accounts Payable Turnover Ratio

Your *Accounts Payable Turnover Ratio* indicates your short-term liquidity.

It answers the question of how frequently your business is paying off its accounts payable during a given period, which gives you insight into how efficiently you are meeting your short-term debts.

$$\text{Accounts Payable Turnover Ratio} = \frac{\text{Total Supply Purchases}}{\left[\text{Beginning Accounts Payable} + \text{Ending Accounts Payable}\right] \div 2}$$

For example, if a business had total supply purchases of $100,000 for the quarter, $20,000 in Accounts Payable at the start of the quarter, and $80,000 in Accounts Payable at the end of the quarter; then its Accounts Payable Turnover Ratio would be 2 for the quarter. This indicates that the business paid off its Accounts Payables two times throughout the quarter.

Unless you receive a discount or benefit, you may not actually want to pay off your Accounts Payable any earlier than necessary. Stretching out your Accounts Payable within the allowed terms is worth considering, if it enables you to use your cash to achieve other higher-yielding outcomes, and provided that you can pay your debts when they fall due.

Accounts Receivable Turnover Ratio

Your *Accounts Receivable Turnover Ratio* indicates how well your business is managing the credit you extend to customers, and how quickly that debt is paid off.

Throughout the COVID crisis, many customers became tardy in meeting their payment obligations. Because your customer credit terms are effectively an interest-free loan, it's important these don't remain outstanding for too long a period of time.

$$\text{Accounts Receivable Turnover Ratio} = \frac{\text{Net Credit Sales}}{\left[\frac{\text{Beginning Accounts Receivable} + \text{Ending Accounts Receivable}}{}\right] \div 2}$$

For example, if a business had net credit sales of $100,000 for the quarter, $5,000 in Accounts Receivable at the start of the quarter, and $15,000 in Accounts Receivable at the end of the quarter; then its Accounts Receivable Turnover Ratio would be 10 for the quarter. This indicates the business converted its receivables to cash 10 times that quarter. This should be compared to previous quarter results for context.

If your Accounts Receivable Turnover Ratio is high, it suggests that debt collection processes are efficient and/or that customers are good at paying their debts on time. If the ratio is low, it suggests the opposite, and you may need to review your account collection processes, credit policies or the creditworthiness of your customers.

Inventory Turnover

Your *Inventory Turnover* indicates the number of days it takes you to sell your stock by seeing how many times you've sold and replaced inventory during a given period.

$$\text{Inventory Turnover} = \frac{\text{Sales}}{\text{Average Inventory}}$$

If a business had monthly sales of $1,000 and an average inventory of $100, then their inventory turnover would be 10. This indicates that the company typically turns over its inventory 10 times per month. It can therefore also be inferred that it takes an average of 3 days (30 days in a month divided by inventory turnover of 10) to clear its inventory.

Using the Inventory Turnover ratio, you're able to make better decisions that affect your inventory stock levels—like purchasing, manufacturing and marketing. For example, having low inventory turnover could indicate an excess of stock or weak sales performance.

Working Capital (Current) Ratio

Your *Current Ratio* tells you the difference between your business' current assets and liabilities. It indicates the health of your business by illuminating its ability to pay its debts with its current assets.

$$\text{Current Ratio} = \frac{\text{Current Assets}}{\text{Current Liabilities}}$$

If your Current Ratio is greater than 1, then your current assets exceed your current liabilities; and you're in a good position to convert those assets to cash quicker, fund your business' operations and pay your short-term liabilities. Remain conscious of your Current Ratio when making any decisions about whether or not to take on additional debt.

Debt to Equity Ratio

Your *Debt to Equity Ratio* tells you how much of your business is being financed with debt, instead of wholly-owned funds. It indicates the ability of your equity to cover the business' debts. The higher the ratio, the higher the risk to you as an equity owner in the business.

$$\text{Debt to Equity Ratio} = \frac{\text{Total Liabilities}}{\text{Total Shareholders' Equity}}$$

During these turbulent times, you'll want to keep an eye on the debt incurred by the business. Ensure that these debts remain serviceable and aren't adding additional stress above and beyond these already trying times.

Wages to Sales Ratio

The *Wages to Sales Ratio* is relevant for retail businesses. It indicates how well sales staff are performing relative to the revenue they generate.

$$\text{Wages to Sales Ratio} = \frac{\text{Wages}}{\text{Gross Sales}} \times 100$$

If each week a business paid \$1,000 in payroll, and sold \$10,000 of products, then its *Wages to Sales Ratio* would be 10. This indicates that the business needs to pay \$10 in payroll to generate \$100 of sales.

You're able to use the Wages to Sales Ratio to compare...

- An individual salesperson's performance over time
- The sales performance of different salespeople
- An individual store's sales performance over time
- The sales performance of different stores
- Total sales performance over different time periods

Armed with this knowledge you may choose to make any number of adjustments. For example, you may adjust which staff you choose to retain or dismiss, select certain stores and/or departments to receive more (or less) support, or choose to customize the trading hours of certain stores in select locations.

Build Sustainability by Managing Your Cash Flow

When thinking about different operating 'modes' a business might experience, we can broadly segment these into one of three realities...

Survival mode   Business-As-Usual mode   Growth mode

In *survival* mode, businesses are looking to batten down the hatches in their efforts to endure through a crisis. In *business-as-usual* mode, businesses continue doing what they've previously done with the expectation of witnessing results not too dissimilar to those from the past. In *growth* mode, businesses are looking to leverage their good current standing and/or favorable market conditions to expand operations in the pursuit of additional profits.

Because of COVID, if you're a business currently operating with a growth mode mentality, then you are one of the lucky few. Most small businesses today find themselves at best resurrecting themselves from the perils of recent survival modes, or at worst wondering if that's even a feasible possibility.

What is *common* to all modes however, is the importance of maintaining good cash flow. Whilst being important for a variety of different reasons, cash flow serves as the lifeblood of your business. Your ultimate pursuit may be profit, but your ability to live another day depends on maintaining adequate cash on hand to keep your head above water.

Good cash flow becomes particularly important during challenging times like these.

Managing your cash flow will help you...

- Apply for loans
- Avoid interest and penalties
- Meet your debt commitments
- Pay your suppliers
- Retain your employees
- Run day-to-day operations

Good cash flow management is your ticket to a sustainable recovery from COVID. You'll want to avoid living hand-to-mouth, since a small unexpected surprise is all it would take to throw a major spanner in the works. Maintaining a positive cash flow is your insurance policy for overcoming any such surprises.

The following are tips for building sustainability into your business by managing your cash flows...

Request More Generous Payment Terms From Suppliers

A natural starting point for improving your cash flow is gaining additional time to pay your suppliers. Despite benefiting you, it is disadvantageous to them. They are under no obligation to extend the courtesy as it's effectively an interest-free loan that comes at *their* own cash flow expense.

Nonetheless, in these post-COVID times, your suppliers need to balance their own cash flow interests against the risk of losing customers because of inflexible payment terms. For some supplier businesses, their priority may be in preventing the latter.

Before making these requests, arm yourself with knowledge of other suppliers' payment terms, to give yourself additional bargaining chips in negotiations and knowing your options if requests are denied.

Promptly Follow-Up Accounts Receivables

Despite your own requests for more generous payment terms, unless you've negotiated extended credit for your customers, now is not the time to be tardy or forgiving with late payment of accounts receivables. Sometimes late payments will be accidental; other times intentional—either way, they negatively impact your business' cash flow.

Without proactive mechanisms in place to identify outstanding invoices, they are likely to slip through the cracks and become a persistent problem. The use of automated reminders (for both you and your customers) will assist in the timely payment of bills, and inform you of risks that impact a positive cash flow balance.

Make it Easy to Get Paid

Eliminate any barriers to getting paid by customers by making it as easy as possible for them to do so. Provide multiple options for making payments. Cater these to the different payment methods available in the market as well as your customers' preferences.

Especially if you're sending invoices online, add a direct payment link to the invoice. This not only adds an additional payment option, but may actually encourage earlier payment too.

Incentivize Quicker Payment With Trade Credit Discounts

Consider offering your customers discounts for paying their invoices faster. This tactic is particularly relevant for businesses that operate with generous margins. You'll need to determine...

What is the *discount?*	What are the *number of days* of the discount period?	What is the *default due date?*
Example: 1%	Example: 10 days	Example: 30 days

Example expressed as "1%/10, Net 30" on your invoice

Ask for Deposits or Use Milestone Payments

Depending on what you sell, there may be a big delay in receiving payment for the goods or services that you provide. This is often the case for service-based businesses where final payment might only be made at the end of a long engagement.

If this applies to you, you may wish to ask your customer for a deposit—say, 50% upfront, and the balance upon delivery. Alternatively, consider breaking up one big payment that would be due at the end of an engagement, into multiple smaller payments to be paid at pre-specified milestones throughout the job.

Maintain Lean Inventory Levels

Maintaining positive cash flow can be challenging when the bulk of your cash is tied up in products that are just sitting on shelves.

Whilst you don't want to jeopardize your ability to satisfy orders as soon as they come through, you ideally want to maintain inventory levels that are just above what is necessary to satisfy order volumes you're likely to receive.

Review historic sales and inventory levels and make sure you're not hoarding additional stock that's just collecting dust on the shelves. If there's a specific product that's in abundance or moving slower than others, consider running a campaign to clear it. You might also consider discontinuing less popular, slow-moving products.

Be Strategic With the Timing of Your Work

For service providers, being strategic with the timing of the jobs that you accept will enable you to better align incoming cash flows with known outgoing expenses.

If there's flexibility on your customers' end, see if they're open to changing the timelines of jobs to better align with cash flow considerations that are impactful to you.

Liquidate Non-Essential Capital Assets

You may have a lot of cash locked up in capital assets; such as office buildings, company cars or production equipment. If cash flow is tight and liquidity is required, consider selling off some of these assets.

Many of these items may no longer be necessary, in which case you've won yourself back a chunk of working capital. In other instances, you could shift from *owning* to *leasing* these assets to free up some cash...

Could you sell your office and start renting or working from co-working space?

Could you sell your car and replace it with corporate fleet rentals?

Could you purchase materials or components currently produced with your own equipment?

You may end up paying more in the long-run, but that may be what's required to keep your head above water for now.

Stocktake Your Operating Expenses

In good times your operating expenses may have gone unchecked, allowing unnecessary costs to potentially fly under the radar.

You may have a hunch that you're overpaying, but the lack of urgency in looking for cost-saving opportunities results in simply doing things the way they've always been done previously—even if that means paying more than you actually need to.

That changes in challenging times like these. The cash flow pressures of COVID should be a trigger for reviewing your operating expenses. Review expenses that relate to your...

- Entertainment
- Insurance
- Marketing
- Office supplies
- Payroll
- Rent
- Repairs and maintenance
- Taxes
- Transportation and travel
- Utilities

You may find opportunities for reducing your costs by considering alternative options from within any of these categories.

Discount High Margin Products to Encourage Additional Sales

An obvious lever for improving your cash flow is to increase your sales. As we all know, this is easier said than done. One quick-fix for a boost to sales is *price discounting*.

The risk of discounting is margin erosion and potential brand damage. Be selective when deciding where in your product mix you will be discounting your prices. A good starting point for identifying which products to discount are those with high margins—the things that cost less to produce but still sell at higher prices...

	◯	△	◻
	Product A	Product B	Product C
Margins:	High	Medium	Low
Production Costs:	$	$$	$$$
Sales Price:	$$$	$$$	$$$
Price Demand Sensitivity:	High	Low	Medium
Price Discounting Brand Damage Sensitivity:	Low	Medium	High

In the example above, *Product A* represents the best candidate for discounting. It has healthy margins, high price demand sensitivity (making discounts more attractive), yet low sensitivity to discounting brand damage.

Understand Debt Finance Options to Carry You Through

If cash flow is tight, as it likely may be, then your business may be searching for a cash boost to help carry it through these difficult times.

You may obtain these extra funds from a variety of sources. At its most basic level, you have two options for sourcing additional cash...

Debt Finance
Borrowing money in the form of loans to be repaid with interest

Equity Finance
Raising money by selling equity in your business

There's no one-size-fits-all approach for deciding what's 'right' for you—different businesses will face different challenges and have access to different funding options.

However, for many businesses confronted with overcoming the challenging impacts of COVID, *debt finance* frequently represents the appropriate and preferable option, with many debt finance tools available for consideration.

Assuming that the cash flow challenges you're experiencing are a specific consequence of COVID, then the remedy you seek should be the *minimum* required for returning back to a path of positive and sustainable cash flow.

To the extent that it's possible, you'll want to retain as much ownership and control over your business. Debt finance affords you that benefit. Equity finance does not.

Going down the equity finance path requires you to share your business' profits with additional shareholders (or additional profits to your existing shareholders). Hopefully, the negative financial impacts of COVID will be short-lived. It would be unfortunate to have a continuing obligation to share the fruits of your business if alternative options can see you through these temporary challenging times.

We also do not know how long these challenges are going to last, or what the 'post-COVID' world is going to look like. Economists, social scientists and medical experts are all uncommitted in their predications on exactly how this all ends and how long that's going to take.

With that being the case, you'll want to retain maximum control over the liabilities that hang over your head. Debt finance provides that luxury—you're in the driver's seat when it comes to making repayments and the timelines that your business needs to repay its debts. Should you find yourself out of 'dangerous waters' sooner than planned, you have the ability to quash outstanding loans at a time of your choosing.

In contrast, making a shareholder disappear is much more challenging and potentially more expensive. This nonetheless needs to be counter-balanced by the fact that debt finance carries with it forced repayment obligations, which equity finance does not.

There are also currently record-low interest rates. Assuming rates remain low—as they are expected to do—debt finance becomes an increasingly attractive option. Low rates may not be a reason alone to take out a loan, but it is a good reason for placing debt finance on a pedestal amongst alternative sources of finance.

As an established business, you are also in a stronger position than a business that's just trying to get off the ground when it comes to receiving a loan from increasingly hesitant lenders.

So, what are the different debt finance options that you should be considering?

Bank Loans

The most common form of debt finance is a *bank loan*. Bank loans enable you to acquire cash upfront in return for repayment of the principal with interest over a period of time.

For this reason, they may be the appropriate solution for helping you weather this storm in the near-term whilst times are particularly tough. They are an especially attractive option with interest rates being as low as they currently are.

If you find yourself experiencing financial hardship as a result of COVID, and have existing loans in place, some banks are also offering flexibility in the form of deferred repayments on eligible loans.

Overdrafts and Lines of Credit

If you find yourself struggling to remain cash flow positive, then overdrafts may prove handy for covering your short-term cash flow shortfalls. If you have a good track record of paying your bills on time and running a profitable business, you may be a candidate for receiving a bank overdraft.

Unlike bank loans, you only pay interest on the amount that's overdrawn, however interest rates are likely to be significantly higher than those of bank loans. They should therefore be considered principally for overcoming short-term cash flow challenges.

Business Credit Cards

Depending on the amount of credit you require, finding a good business credit card may be the most practical and pragmatic option. With a bit of research, try find a card that combines…

Low fees

Long interest-free periods

Low interest rates

If you're looking for something to get you through temporary cash flow challenges, a business credit card may be a good option.

Loans From Family and Friends

When done with sensitivity to the relationship, and repaid without complication, loans from family or friends can be a very attractive option. They typically have…

- Minimal admin or credit checks involved
- The possibility of zero (or very low) interest rates
- Flexible repayment terms

Loans from family and friends are normally for smaller sums of money. This means they may be appropriate for addressing short-term cash flow challenges (but less appropriate for a big asset purchase).

Be aware though, that if things don't work out entirely as planned, these loans run the risk of souring relationships with the friend or family lender.

Self-Funding

One option always at your disposal is loaning the business money from yourself. This is different to putting more *equity* into the business.

To properly loan the business money, you'll need to draw up formal legal loan documents that make it clear that the cash injection is *not* to be misconstrued as an equitable contribution—but rather a loan—just like any other instrument of debt.

There are tax benefits in providing personal funds in the form of debt over equity. Providing a personal self-funded loan to your business will also make it easier to get the money out of your business and back into your pockets as soon as it's safe or desirable to do so.

Supplier Trade Credit

You may not think of trade credit in the same way you do a bank loan, but if short-term cash flow constraints are your principle challenge, they may be the logical starting point.

Trade credit is an agreement between your business and one of its suppliers, for them to provide you with goods or services that typically only need to be paid 30 to 90 days later, and with no interest or additional charges.

Access to generous payment terms have become increasingly difficult as *all* businesses address their *own* COVID-related cash flow challenges. However, your request will be weighed against the risk of losing you as a customer if flexible terms are not provided. If cash flow is a challenge for your business, you have little to lose in asking.

Retail Store Credit

Despite current financial pressures, you may still need to make necessary purchases for your business; like new technology, furniture or office supplies. Some retail stores offer store credit via partnerships with third-party finance companies.

These credits allow you to buy now, pay later. Payments are broken down into installments, which alleviates cash flow burdens of a big upfront outlay. So long as you're able to meet your repayments on time, you won't get slogged with paying the (often high) interest charges.

Equipment Finance

Sometimes the cash you require is for the specific purpose of acquiring new equipment for the business, rather than to address general cash flow challenges. Because of COVID, you may for example be seeking to alter your product mix, and this may involve the purchase of new business equipment. If this is the case, consider...

Hire Purchase Arrangements
...whereby you own the equipment and repay it in installments with interest over a period of time; or

Equipment Leasing
...whereby the lender owns the equipment and you rent it from them, with the option of buying it at the end of the lease

Asset Refinancing

Although also a form of equipment finance, *asset refinancing* works differently and has a different purpose. It works by using your business' existing assets (e.g. buildings, equipment, vehicles, etc.) as security for a loan. In the event that you default on your loan repayments, the lender takes the asset away from you.

In contrast to other forms of equipment finance, its purpose is to free up cash in the short term, as opposed to providing the funds to purchase new equipment. It is therefore a useful option if seeking a short-term cash flow solution.

Invoice Financing

Consider using invoice financing (also known as *factoring*) as another source of short-term finance. This involves selling your accounts receivable to a third-party financier at a discounted rate. They take ownership of the outstanding invoice and you receive payment earlier (from the financier) than the payment terms stated on the invoice.

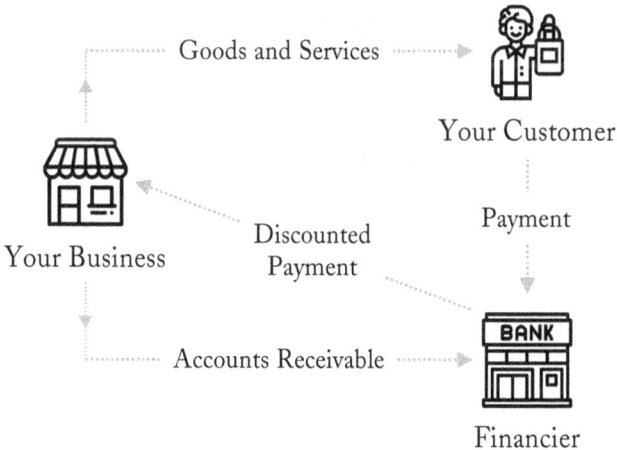

Goods and Services

Your Customer

Your Business

Discounted Payment

Payment

Accounts Receivable

BANK

Financier

Government Assistance Measures to Help You Out

Governments have a vested interest in supporting small businesses navigate their way out of the COVID crisis. Small businesses are the backbone of many economies and account for a disproportionate share of production and employment.

For this reason, many governments have introduced a number of COVID stimuli responses aimed specifically at alleviating many of the financial hardships experienced by small businesses as a result of the virus. These responses attempt to provide businesses with financial support to see them through these challenging times.

These programs, initiatives and incentives are administered via different government agencies, but frequently involve the local tax authority. Measures are normally geared around four overarching goals, all of which are necessary for the functioning of a healthy economy...

Business solvency	Cash flow support	Employee retention	Growth & investment

The following are some common government-sponsored assistance measures intended to help small businesses persist through challenges created by COVID. Consider if any are relevant to your circumstances and exist within your jurisdiction.

Tax Relief

Tax authorities offer a range of tax relief options to small businesses. Where they exist, these often take the form of tailored solutions for individual businesses. For example, your business may be...

Granted a temporary reduction or deferral of tax payments or withholdings owed throughout the year

Able to change the frequency of its VAT or GST reporting cycle to get faster access to tax refunds

Eligible for payroll or land tax relief

There may also be added leniency in holding directors personally liable for tax debts owed by the business.

Wage Subsidies and Paycheck Protection Programs

Because of COVID, many businesses were forced to layoff employees. As a result, some governments introduced wage subsidies or provided disaster loans to give businesses cash to pay their employees. These programs enable employers to keep paying their employees even if they were stood down, so that they're able to quickly return back to work when circumstances permit.

To receive these subsidies, the business needs to demonstrate a significant shortfall in turnover. Recipient employees typically needed to be permanent full-time, part-time or long-term casuals engaged on a regular and systematic basis in the leadup to COVID. In some instances, employees that were initially stood down but then re-hired will also be eligible.

Employee Retention Tax Credits

In addition to wage subsidies, some governments are offering employee retention tax credits to encourage businesses to keep their employees.

These are refundable tax credits that are applied against payroll taxes, equal to a percentage of the qualified wages that an eligible employer pays their employees.

Where they exist, they typically only apply to businesses that have experienced a significant reduction in revenue, or were subject to a government-mandated suspension of business.

Cash Flow Boosts

Some governments are providing temporary cash flow support to businesses in the form of tax-free cash flow boosts, delivered through credits to the business' tax withholdings on eligible payments, like income payments. Credits are normally received with the same frequency that the business lodges its tax withholding documents.

Where they exist, cash flow boosts normally require no new forms to be completed—they are automatically calculated and applied by the relevant tax authority.

Increases to Instant Asset Write-Off Thresholds

In an effort to promote business investment, some tax authorities have increased their instant asset write-off thresholds and/or softened their eligibility criteria so that larger businesses can now apply too.

If this applies to you, your business could claim immediate deductions (up to a capped amount) for certain asset purchases like vehicles, tools and office equipment.

Thresholds normally apply on a *per asset basis*, so eligible businesses have the option of writing-off multiple assets.

Acceleration of Asset Depreciation Deductions

Some tax authorities have accelerated the timeframes with which asset depreciation deductions may be claimed.

Where they exist, tax benefits for eligible assets are expeditiously triggered upon *installation* or *first use,* instead of a later date. Existing depreciation rules typically still also apply to the balance of the asset's cost too.

These deductions will apply to eligible assets acquired *after* the announcement date of any such initiatives, and where the asset was installed or first used before the specified sunset date of the program.

Access to Pension Funds

In some jurisdictions, governments have permitted individuals to access a portion of their pension or superannuation fund.

Whilst it is only individuals (not businesses) that are able to do this, these measures may help business owners keep cash in their business for the purpose of maintaining positive cash flow and to avoid withdrawing funds for their own personal short-term needs.

Insolvency Protections

Some governments have temporarily increased the threshold at which a creditor is able to issue a statutory demand on a business, as well as the time that that businesses has to respond. These protections are often also accompanied by temporary relief for directors from any personal liability for trading whilst insolvent.

Relief for Commercial Tenants

With government-mandated lockdowns, many small businesses faced the grim reality that rent was still owed, even if shops remained closed. To address this, some governments have placed a temporary hold on evictions and lease terminations for commercial tenants, applying to businesses unable to meet rent commitments due to COVID.

Where rent relief exists, reductions are normally commensurate with the tenant's decline in turnover. Rent relief principles are typically expressed in a mandatory Code of Conduct or enacted via legislation.

Utilities Payment Support

Just like rent, utility bills persist even in the absence of sales. Many electricity, gas and water providers have a *financial hardship* policy that includes payment extensions and allow for tailored payment plans.

To address financial stress caused by COVID, some governments have also introduced measures that prevent utility providers from disconnecting their customers, as well as deferring referrals from the utility company to debt collection agencies or credit default listings.

Case Study: Accounting and Finance

Context

Natalie runs an Italian restaurant.

When COVID hit, she was forced to shut her doors to customers for in-dining experiences. This lasted for two months.

Upon re-opening, she was limited to allowing no more than 30 customers into the restaurant—less than half the restaurant's capacity.

Throughout all this time, Natalie provided take-away and food delivery services, however these represented only 20% of average annual revenue.

All of this placed large strain on her cash flow, and jeopardizes her restaurant's ongoing viability.

Actions

Natalie creates budgets and forecasts that utilize 'best', 'base' and 'worst'-case assumptions that are specific to her post-COVID realities.

Her research reveals a growing consumer preference for food delivery services, and earmarks this as a prioritized driver of revenue.

She better-acquaints herself with cash flow KPIs—like her Operating Cash Flow, and Accounts Payable and Receivable Turnover Ratios. She also analyzes the ongoing commercial viability of her restaurant, by considering its Gross and Net Profit Margins.

Natalie requests an additional 30 days to pay her long-term suppliers. Half of them approve her request. She also changes her ordering patterns to only order enough non-perishables to satisfy two weeks' (not four) worth of operations.

She takes out a line of credit with her bank, as well as formally loans the business some of her own money.

Natalie is also granted tax relief, wage subsidies and a cash flow boost from the government.

Results

Natalie's restaurant has become a leading food delivery service in her local area. Food deliveries now account for half of monthly revenue, aligning with her best-case scenario forecasts.

She has even hired a delivery driver and currently rents a car to facilitate deliveries. Now that the restaurant can operate at full capacity, she is making more money than ever before.

The restaurant is once again cash flow positive, and able to return to the original payment terms of all of her suppliers.

Conclusion

Over the last few months, the words "unprecedented times" have been dropped into conversations more frequently than anyone would dare quantify. The reality however, is that in many ways—at least from a business perspective—these are *not* unprecedented times.

What *is* unprecedented are the novel circumstances that made the impacts of the COVID-19 pandemic unique: our integrated and inter-dependent world. The forces of globalization mean that no *one* country, business or individual was sheltered from its consequences.

What is *not* unprecedented are the pressures on business to respond to an external event that existentially threatens its continued viability. The coronavirus is far from the first time that businesses were dealt an unwelcomed hand and forced to rebound in an unfavorable climate.

It is tempting to catastrophize the situation. There are no guarantees on how and when it all ends. The closest we come, is knowing that at some point, it will. Most businesses will lament on the adversity of their reality. This is fair, but unhelpful.

Shrewd businesses will use this time to transform. They will see the positives of the moment, and flip the *troubles* of today into the *opportunities* of tomorrow.

Across all businesses, there remain a plenitude of initiatives able to be adopted for rising above the current challenges of today. And just as the times are 'unprecedented' for the scale and speed that damage was inflicted, so too can that scale and speed shift those same businesses to better and brighter places.

Business improvements are often spawned in the most unlikely of times. Or maybe it's exactly because of those times that such improvements take place.

When backed into a corner, survival implores new and better ways of doing things. Many of these things may have been on the backburner for a while, but COVID elevated their priority from *nice-to-haves* into *need-to-haves*.

Moving forward, many of these initiatives will become part of your standard modus operandi. They will enable you to run a more effective and efficient business. And although it would have been preferable implementing them under stable conditions or timelines of your own choosing, their fruits nonetheless will prove equally sweet.

Your business has been burnt, yet you choose to plough on. Through your commitment to persevere, you'll emerge victorious on the other end. You will have adopted new perspectives, developed new capabilities and become a more resourceful and resilient business. Recovering from this crisis will be a de-facto up-skilling of sorts, that will hold you in good stead through future challenges and better times too.

Never let a good crisis go to waste...

Initiatives Summary

We've covered a lot of initiatives throughout this book. It's easy to feel overwhelmed by the enormity of the job in coming back from COVID.

Instead of feeling burdened by the weight of initiatives, feel relieved by the multitude of pathways that exist for building your post-COVID recovery strategy.

Across the following pages, we summarize the different initiatives discussed throughout the book.

⚒ Marketing and Sales

Understand Your New Customers With Buyer Personas

- ❑ Understand the attributes you're looking to capture
- ❑ Build multiple personas for different customer profiles
- ❑ Conduct customer interviews
- ❑ Involve your team
- ❑ Undertake independent research
- ❑ Aggregate your research and interviews
- ❑ Build a solid template
- ❑ Humanize the abstract
- ❑ Be specific
- ❑ Embed into your business

Target Customers With Inbound Marketing Tactics

- ❑ Identify your target audiences with buyer personas
- ❑ Conduct a content audit
- ❑ Identify your 'watering holes'
- ❑ Determine your content release timelines
- ❑ Map out your consolidated inbound marketing strategy
- ❑ Develop great content
- ❑ Back your content up with strong call-to-actions
- ❑ Deliver (and syndicate) your content
- ❑ Repurpose your content
- ❑ Nurture your leads

Expedite Results With Pay Per Click Advertising

- ❑ Find the right keywords
- ❑ Make use of 'negative' keywords
- ❑ Select the optimal match types
- ❑ Create good ad copy
- ❑ Develop multiple ads
- ❑ Select the right bid strategy
- ❑ Target specific demographics
- ❑ Use geo-targeting
- ❑ Take advantage of device targeting
- ❑ Use call campaigns to encourage immediate contact

Reacquaint Yourself With Your Sales Pipeline

- ❏ Define your pipeline stages
- ❏ Prioritize your opportunities
- ❏ Weed out opportunities unlikely to convert
- ❏ Update your pipeline tracking tools frequently
- ❏ Track relevant opportunity information
- ❏ Build a sales dashboard
- ❏ Automate elements of your sales processes
- ❏ Run regular sales pipeline meetings
- ❏ Become perpetually fixated with next steps
- ❏ Use as a cash flow forecasting tool

Develop Repeatable Results With Sales Playbooks

- ❏ Involve the whole team
- ❏ Transfer knowledge out of the heads of individuals
- ❏ Standardize your best practices
- ❏ Right-size your playbooks
- ❏ Collate all of your existing marketing and sales collateral
- ❏ Map your sales process to the customer's buying cycle
- ❏ Use for onboarding
- ❏ Support with training
- ❏ Promote adoption and ease of access
- ❏ Update periodically

Product

Optimize Your Product Mix

- ❑ Be clear on your goals
- ❑ Review your existing product mix
- ❑ Understand your production costs
- ❑ Consider your brand and reputation
- ❑ Reconcile short term and long term goals
- ❑ Expand or contract based on balancing considerations
- ❑ Consider natural product lifecycles
- ❑ Scrutinize margins in addition to sales volumes
- ❑ Consider implications to messaging and positioning
- ❑ Productize your services

Maximize Profits With a Product Pricing Strategy

- ❑ Adjust your pricing to new market realities
- ❑ Communicate your value
- ❑ Get customers hooked
- ❑ Calculate the lifetime value of your customers
- ❑ Reduce your costs to pass on savings
- ❑ Utilize loss leader products
- ❑ Bundle offerings for additional value
- ❑ Offer installment payment plans
- ❑ Provide discounts for cash and early payments
- ❑ Create tiered pricing across your product mix

Re-Build Your Brand

- ❑ Determine your reason for being
- ❑ Decide what makes you, *you*
- ❑ Figure out your most important values
- ❑ Consider how you want to be regarded
- ❑ Crystalize the things your customers expect from you
- ❑ Carve out your coveted place in the market
- ❑ Be authentic
- ❑ Appreciate that branding is a team effort
- ❑ Run a disciplined process to re-build the brand
- ❑ Put your personality on display

Improve Your Offering With Better Customer Feedback

- ☐ Monitor feedback on digital channels
- ☐ Talk to your customers
- ☐ Specifically contact past customers
- ☐ Speak with key team members
- ☐ Request immediate feedback after purchase
- ☐ Conduct surveys
- ☐ Gain feedback with incentives
- ☐ Tap visitors to your website
- ☐ Review your web analytics
- ☐ Simply watch and observe

Cost-Effectively Differentiate Yourself on Quality

- ☐ Get on the front-foot with customer-centricity
- ☐ Integrate quality into your business' culture and training
- ☐ Set measurable standards and benchmarks
- ☐ Develop a Quality Management System
- ☐ Familiarize yourself with your products
- ☐ Test products and get feedback from real customers
- ☐ Personally inspect your key product processes
- ☐ Improve quality via customer issues and complaints
- ☐ Deploy technology and upgrades to uphold quality standards
- ☐ Review results and make continuous improvements

📈 Growth

Go Deeper and Broader in New and Current Markets
- ☐ Fix your 'leaking bucket'
- ☐ Determine the markets with room to grow
- ☐ Conduct rigorous market research
- ☐ Understand new target customer profiles
- ☐ Leverage your competitive advantages
- ☐ Identify new distribution opportunities
- ☐ Consider your product mix
- ☐ Offer pricing incentives
- ☐ Identify your points of differentiation
- ☐ Evolve a product

Win New Customers Through Referrals
- ☐ Establish a formal customer referral program
- ☐ Set goals and targets
- ☐ Make referring easy to do
- ☐ Incentivize for referrals
- ☐ Time the request
- ☐ Give and take
- ☐ Maintain multiple touchpoints with those that are referred
- ☐ Make sharing your content easy
- ☐ Prepare yourself for new customers
- ☐ Say thank you

Increase Share of Wallet Through Cross-Selling and Upselling
- ☐ Determine your motivations
- ☐ Prioritize upselling
- ☐ Incentivize and reward
- ☐ Explain not just *what*, but *why* you recommend
- ☐ Time your recommendations
- ☐ Offer encouraging pricing
- ☐ Maintain relevance in your marketing
- ☐ Only offer relevant recommendations
- ☐ Start doing re-marketing
- ☐ Help. Don't hinder.

Optimize Your Website to Win, Grow and Retain Customers

- ❑ Keep it simple, clean and professional
- ❑ Communicate key information
- ❑ Make your website multi-device friendly
- ❑ Add social proof
- ❑ Ensure it's easy to get in touch
- ❑ Offer incentives and discounts
- ❑ Share great content
- ❑ Incorporate back into your holistic marketing strategy
- ❑ Review your web analytics
- ❑ Add live chat

Growth Through Partnerships and Strategic Alliances

- ❑ Recognize that it's not an alternative to hiring
- ❑ Determine your strengths and weaknesses
- ❑ Identify good partners
- ❑ Clarify the purpose and goals of the partnership
- ❑ Be clear on roles, responsibilities and accountabilities
- ❑ Intervene early on issues
- ❑ Always be learning and adapting
- ❑ Create a relationship of honesty
- ❑ Clarify how the fruits of the partnership will be distributed
- ❑ Ensure you're appropriately legally set-up

⚙️ Operations

Update Your Business Plan to Reflect New Realities
- ☐ Executive Summary
- ☐ Business Description
- ☐ Market Analysis
- ☐ Organization and Management
- ☐ Products and Services
- ☐ Sales and Marketing
- ☐ Operations Plan
- ☐ Funding Request
- ☐ Financial Plan
- ☐ Appendix

Improve Your Processes to Achieve Efficiency Gains
- ☐ Identify opportunities for process improvements
- ☐ Document the existing steps
- ☐ Brainstorm improvements with a focus on automation
- ☐ Gain input from key stakeholders
- ☐ Draft updated processes
- ☐ Educate and gain buy-in
- ☐ Create a home for your processes
- ☐ Ensure required infrastructure and resources are in place
- ☐ Share pre-activation communications
- ☐ Review and adapt

Revise Your Organizational Structure for Smooth Operations
- ☐ Revise your organizational structure for smooth operations
- ☐ Align to your strategy
- ☐ Consult your team
- ☐ Prioritize a decentralized chain of command
- ☐ Determine how you would like decisions to be made
- ☐ Prioritize *pragmatism* over *process*
- ☐ Stocktake the talent within your team
- ☐ Understand the jobs to be done
- ☐ Ensure workloads are balanced
- ☐ Document responsibilities and accountabilities
- ☐ Create career progression pathways

Make Meetings Matter

- ❑ Perform a stocktake of your existing meetings
- ❑ Clarify the core elements of each meeting
- ❑ Document the meeting's *purpose, participants* and *structure*
- ❑ Allocate a meeting owner
- ❑ Eliminate distractions
- ❑ Enforce pre-meeting preparation requirements
- ❑ Ensure meetings run to an agenda
- ❑ Keep meetings short
- ❑ Document action items, commitments and next steps
- ❑ Avoid scope creep

Improve Internal Communications to Recognize New Realities

- ❑ Employ active listening
- ❑ Determine if a meeting is actually necessary
- ❑ Avoid email if appropriate
- ❑ Write better emails
- ❑ Ask better questions
- ❑ Utilize videoconferencing and project management technologies
- ❑ Develop an email sorting system
- ❑ Promote proactive bottom-up communications
- ❑ Batch-process questions and discussions
- ❑ Invest in knowledge repositories

🏛 Team

Improve Results Through Better Performance Management
- ❏ Understand that the goalposts have moved
- ❏ Increase performance management intervention frequency
- ❏ Keep performance management 'forward-focused'
- ❏ Don't forget to find the *good*
- ❏ Individualize performance expectations
- ❏ Have a conversation around KPIs
- ❏ Explicitly recognize good performance
- ❏ Promote job security
- ❏ Introduce performance gamification
- ❏ Make performance management about teams too

Drive Employee Engagement With Reward and Recognition
- ❏ Recognize both formally and informally
- ❏ Embrace rising stars by expediting their career trajectories
- ❏ Reward *values* and *behaviors* too
- ❏ Introduce a performance-based bonus incentive scheme
- ❏ Share positive customer feedback
- ❏ Promote peer recognition
- ❏ Use gamification
- ❏ Keep records
- ❏ Recognize and reward across the entire team
- ❏ Separate praise from criticism

Become a Business Your Team Enjoys Working For
- ❏ Promote work-life balance
- ❏ Celebrate the wins
- ❏ Make social media... Social
- ❏ Create a harmonizing work environment
- ❏ Provide small perks and treats
- ❏ Promote structured fun and socialization
- ❏ Create exercise opportunities and provide wellness gestures
- ❏ Encourage the taking of short breaks
- ❏ Make the most of the holidays
- ❏ Celebrate birthdays, anniversaries and key milestones

Maximize Productivity With Flexible Work Arrangements

- ☐ Maximize productivity with flexible work arrangements
- ☐ Have your team create a quiet space
- ☐ Set up appropriate home workstations
- ☐ Increase the frequency of check-ins
- ☐ Separate work time from personal time
- ☐ Ensure a good internet connection and address IT security
- ☐ Set daily agendas
- ☐ Encourage the team to get out of the house
- ☐ Be cautious when it comes to multitasking
- ☐ Maintain a physical presence
- ☐ Exchange extended work hours for Time Off In Lieu

Motivate Through Non-Financial Incentives and Benefits

- ☐ Utilize public recognition events
- ☐ Institute rostered days off
- ☐ Grant extra annual leave
- ☐ Provide gifts as a show of thanks
- ☐ Facilitate time with management
- ☐ Enable leadership opportunities
- ☐ Create time for passion projects
- ☐ Support professional development opportunities
- ☐ Offer flexible work arrangements
- ☐ Allow flexible work hours

Accounting and Finance

Prepare for the Future With Budgeting and Forecasting Tools

- ❑ Utilize both *budgets* and *forecasts*
- ❑ Be discerning when extrapolating from past assumptions
- ❑ Undertake complementary independent research
- ❑ Involve your team
- ❑ Record your assumptions
- ❑ Create a dynamic tool
- ❑ Track your budgets to actuals
- ❑ Identify drivers of revenue
- ❑ Model for best, base and worst-case scenarios
- ❑ Make better business decisions

Stay on Track With Key Performance Indicators

- ❑ Operating Cash Flow
- ❑ Gross Profit Margin
- ❑ Net Profit Margin
- ❑ Revenue Growth Rate
- ❑ Accounts Payable Turnover Ratio
- ❑ Accounts Receivable Turnover Ratio
- ❑ Inventory Turnover
- ❑ Working Capital (Current) Ratio
- ❑ Debt to Equity Ratio
- ❑ Wages to Sales Ratio

Build Sustainability by Managing Your Cash Flow

- ❑ Request more generous payment terms from suppliers
- ❑ Promptly follow-up accounts receivables
- ❑ Make it easy to get paid
- ❑ Incentivize quicker payment with trade credit discounts
- ❑ Ask for deposits or use milestone payments
- ❑ Maintain lean inventory levels
- ❑ Be strategic with the timing of your work
- ❑ Liquidate non-essential capital assets
- ❑ Stocktake your operating expenses
- ❑ Discount high margin products to encourage additional sales

Understand Debt Finance Options to Carry You Through

- ❑ Bank loans
- ❑ Overdrafts and Lines of credit
- ❑ Business credit cards
- ❑ Loans from family and friends
- ❑ Self-funding
- ❑ Supplier trade credit
- ❑ Retail store credit
- ❑ Equipment finance
- ❑ Asset refinancing
- ❑ Invoice financing

Government Assistance Measures to Help You Out

- ❑ Tax relief
- ❑ Wage subsidies and paycheck protection programs
- ❑ Employee retention tax credits
- ❑ Cash flow boosts
- ❑ Increases to instant asset write-off thresholds
- ❑ Acceleration of asset depreciation deductions
- ❑ Access to pension funds
- ❑ Insolvency protections
- ❑ Relief for commercial tenants
- ❑ Utilities payment support

For further assistance in helping your business come back from COVID, visit **comingbackfromcovid.com**

Disclaimer

All information provided in this book is provided "as is" and with no warranties. No express or implied warranties of any type, including for example implied warranties of merchantability or fitness for a particular purpose, are made with respect to the information, or any use of the information, within this book. Evian Gutman makes no representations and extends no warranties of any type as to the accuracy or completeness of any information or content within this book.

Evian Gutman specifically disclaims liability for incidental or consequential damages and assumes no responsibility or liability for any loss or damage suffered by any person as a result of the use, misuse or reliance of any of the information or content contained within this book.

If seeking further clarity on issues, readers should consult a lawyer, tax and accounting professional if they are unsure of anything.

www.ingramcontent.com/pod-product-compliance
Lightning Source LLC
Chambersburg PA
CBHW031842200326
41597CB00012B/234